*Dedicated to the men, women
and children who sow the seeds,
tend the crops and livestock
and harvest the land's bounty
on farms all across this great country.*

——■——

My Folks
AND THE
Family Farm

A Treasury of Farm Stories
Submitted by Readers of Capper's *and* Grit

Capper Press
Topeka, Kansas

Editor
Samantha Adams

Assistant to the Editor
Patricia Thompson

Production and Illustrations
Bruce Bealmear

ISBN: 0-941678-51-2

FOREWORD

Truck farms and thank-you-ma'ams, box suppers and licking the dasher. If these words evoke clear images in your mind, chances are you've spent at least part of your life on a farm. Whether you called the farm home or just remember your annual summer visits to Grandma and Grandpa's acreage, you are likely to recall your time there as an enriching, character-building experience. The latest *My Folks* book celebrates the hard work, the community spirit, the fun, the hardships and the sense of family closeness that were all integral ingredients of life on the family farm.

My Folks and the Family Farm is the eighth volume in the *My Folks* series, which includes: *My Folks Came in a Covered Wagon, My Folks Claimed the Plains, My Folks and the One-Room Schoolhouse, My Folks' Depression Days, My Folks and the Civil War, My Folks and World War II* and *My Folks and the Land of Opportunity*. The opinions expressed are those of people who have experienced farm life first hand. We make no claim to complete historical accuracy; minimal spelling, grammar and punctuation corrections were made to facilitate comprehension while maintaining the authors' spirit and style.

The majority of today's farms are larger, more specialized operations. They may run more efficiently, but they lack the spirit of self sufficiency that arose from farms where families raised or grew everything on their table. The heyday of those farms may have passed, but the legacy they fostered lives on. As long as there are those who remember and pass on the feelings of kinship and accomplishment they experienced while working together to make a living from the land, the intergenerational bonds of the family farm will live on.

Samantha Adams
Editor

CONTENTS

Chapter 1: The Many Sides of Farm Life

I Remember the Watermelons

I remember my grandparents' 320-acre farm in south-central Kansas. My grandparents are gone now, but I remember those good times we had on the farm.

There was no running water in the house. It was carried in from a windmill a short distance from the house. Meals were cooked on an old wood-burning stove. The kitchen had a cabinet with a flour bin. The dining room had a wood-burning stove.

My uncle and his three children lived with us, as did my unmarried aunt, who did much of the cooking. There were family reunions with aunts, uncles and cousins. Meals were eaten on a long table that seated 12 to 14. Those who couldn't sit at the table grabbed a plate and ate wherever they could. The food was delicious.

We raised crops, and I especially remember the watermelons. We cousins would go to the field and burst open a melon and eat it right there. There were also sand plums and wild grapes, which made good jelly.

We played games outside. We'd take a wagon and go to a distant hill and ride down the hill in the wagon. We used a wagon wheel for a merry-go-round.

My grandparents were hard-working people. I remember Grandma in her ankle-length dresses and Grandpa relaxing in his special recliner chair.

Helen Stoddard
Cambridge, Kansas

Growing Up Near U.S. Route 30

The brick house where I was born in 1923 and grew up in was built in 1853 and 1854 by my great-grandfather. He lived in Connecticut as a small boy; later he came to Indiana from Ohio in 1838. His family originally came from England. My mother, who died at the age of 83, spent most of her life in the brick home.

The road going past our house, which went between the house and the barn, was originally an old trail. A friend whose family lived in a small town a few miles from our home tells this story. His father told him that when they went to the county seat, a distance of about 12 miles from their home, they stopped at my great-grandparents and stayed all night before completing the trip. The first Route 30 was paved in 1919 or 1920. Before that time travel was mostly horse and buggy or wagons. One winter, ice accumulated to a great depth on the pavement. Neighbor boys put on ice skates and skated right on the highway. There was little or no traffic. Early automobiles were often put up on blocks for the winter months. There was little road repair equipment. The county roads were often cared for by farmers who worked out their taxes using their team of horses. When cars became more plentiful and Greyhound buses went past our place, you could catch the bus and ride into town or even to the bigger city.

Dad owned 123 acres of ground during this time. Farming with horses, he had to have help. He did have an early tractor, but I don't know what year he got it. We had a succession of hired men during the summers and sometimes all year. Sometimes Dad would hire a man who came in off the highway. They usually stayed the night. I remember some of the extra things they did in the evenings. One man carved animals and so forth from nutshells and small pieces of wood. Some would bring candy for us kids when he got to go into town. One even brought candy to Mother.

There were many things for kids to see and learn, because Route 30 was then a national highway. Mom fed a lot of tramps. Everybody was afraid they would do damage if you didn't give them something to eat. She usually asked them to sit on the porch swing to eat. Dad seldom let anyone sleep in the barn.

Many of the hobos smoked, and it was dangerous to let them stay in a barn with hay and straw. Some of them would offer to work for food. Mother fed one man who said he wanted to mow our yard. You have never seen such a mess as he made of it. He mowed in circles and every which way. I think Mom asked him to stop. Occasionally someone we didn't know got to sleep in the house. I remember one man who was supposed to be crawling across the United States. He had pictures of himself with wooden blocks for his hands and knees. He only traveled at night, and we never knew whether he really did this or not. I don't think he ever got in *Ripley's Believe It or Not*.

We had to cross the busy highway many times a day. For a number of years the milk cows were driven across to pasture and back, morning and night. Dad had a stop sign, and the whole family would help. I don't remember any cattle being killed, but at least one was injured. The crossing was below the crest of a hill and very dangerous. As traffic became heavier and faster, it was a real hazard. After the three children left home, Mother and Dad drove the cattle through the creek bed for a while.

At the corner of Route 30 and the little road that ran behind the house—the back road—stood a huge elm tree. There are now no trees near here of such size and fullness as that one. Orioles made several of their hanging nests in it every year, as did many other birds. It was so dense that rain barely went through it, and you could stand beneath it during a rainstorm and not get wet. I remember Dad driving the team and a wagon loaded with hay under it until the rain let up; then he proceeded to the barn. I well remember the day they cut down the old elm tree. Everybody was told to stay in the house while they dynamited the stump.

Route 30 no longer goes past the old brick house, which is still standing. The road is still there, but Route 30 was moved several miles away.

Betty J. Anderson
Columbia City, Indiana

From Rags to Riches

The heating stove—to the magic of a thermostat.
The rain barrel—to abundant tap water.
The cellar—to temperature-controlled refrigerators.
The horse and buggy—to the luxury of the automobile.
The Missouri mud roads—to super highways.
The old party line—to world-wide communications.
The railroad train—to the stupendous jet plane.
The straw broom—to the powerful vacuum cleaner.
The manual typewriter—to the mysterious computer.
The old cookstove—to the convenience of a microwave.
Home-cooked meals—to repulsive TV dinners.
The outhouse—to the pleasure of a flush toilet.
Battery-powered radios—to wonderful television.
Home movie cameras—to camcorders and VCR tapes.
The one-room schoolhouse—to crowded city schools.
The village doctor—to specialized medicine.
Simple home remedies—to expensive pharmacies.
The small-town general store—to Sam's Wal-Mart.
The pantry—to the gigantic supermarket.
Do it yourself—to the lifelike robot.
Dresses and petticoats—to acceptable ladies' pants.
Natural beauty—to Avon and Mary Kay.
The feather bed—to the comfort of an innerspring mattress.
Human ingenuity—to numerous push buttons.
The treadle sewing machine—to the marvelous serger.
The no-key doors—to the sophisticated home security system.
The team of horses—to a dependable tractor.
The written word—to a recorded tape.
The lowly washboard—to the wonderful automatic washer.
The backyard clothesline—to the lint-free dryer.

Auda B. Bratcher
Raytown, Missouri

The Roedel Farm

The Roedel farm was originally purchased from the State of Michigan on January 3, 1854, by William Ladd. He sold it to William Wenn on July 8, 1856, who sold it to James Applebee on November 13, 1857. We have the original deed from the State of Michigan.

On January 29, 1866, James Applebee sold the farm to John L. Roedel. The land at that time was covered with virgin timber.

John L. Roedel Sr., with his wife, Margaretha, nee Ortner, came to America from Oberwurmbach, Germany, in April of 1852. At that time they had four children, including John Leonard Roedel Jr., who was 12 weeks old when they came to Frankenmuth, Michigan. When John L. Roedel Jr. was 29 years old, he purchased the farm from his father, built a house and brought his bride, Barbara Geyer, to this farm. They had six children: three sons and three daughters. The oldest son left the farm to make his fortune in the city, but the other two sons farmed for a living. Three daughters also married farmers.

John Roedel Jr. sold the farm to his youngest son, Otto, on April 18, 1921. Otto brought his bride, Linda Fischer, to the farm on May 29, 1921. They also had six children: three sons and three daughters. One son and one daughter died in childhood. One daughter married a farmer and the other daughter became a nurse. Both of the remaining sons became farmers. During the years of Otto's farming, he had a bit of everything—cows, pigs, sheep and chickens. He raised crops to feed the livestock and some crops for cash. Of the 74-acre farm, 20 acres were left in timber so that there would be enough wood to heat the house for generations to come.

Otto Roedel sold the farm to his youngest son, Howard, and his wife, Grace, nee Hecht, on May 2, 1955. At that time they were the parents of three girls.

Howard and Grace farmed the Roedel homestead for 35 years until Howard's death in September of 1990. During our years of farming we cleared the 20 acres of woods. Today the house is heated with natural gas. We had a dairy operation until March of 1980, a beef operation until the fall of 1988, and then we raised cash crops, including sugar beets, corn, wheat, soybeans, hay and oats. Through the years our daughters were a big help on the farm, but all have their own homes now. The youngest daughter, Joy, and her husband, Larry Kischnick, live in the farmhouse that was built by Joy's great-grandfather, John L. Roedel Jr., in 1881. Their two daughters, Erin and Leah, have the distinct honor of being the fifth generation to live in the same house.

The farm has been in the Roedel family for more than 125 years. We are thankful to our good Lord for letting this happen. We also hope that the farm will remain in the family for many years to come.

Grace Roedel

Frankenmuth, Michigan

Sharing Stories of the Past

My grandparents, John Milton Hardman and Martha Isabell Hardman, came to Kansas with four children from Milton, Iowa, in 1878 and homesteaded south of Lenora in Graham County. They built a sod house with a cellar beneath. They planted an orchard of apples and pears and planted garden vegetables and potatoes.

They farmed corn and sorghum and had a herd of milk cows. They were successful, with all the family working and sharing the farm work.

As their family was growing, they built a stone house with three large rooms. From 1879 to 1890 five boys were born, making nine living children in the family.

My grandfather kept and raised driving horses. He owned a breeding horse called a stud. Each son received a buggy and team of horses as they grew up, for buggies, surreys, spring wagons and plain old wagons were the transportation of the day. My grandfather also held stud services for horses in the county, as everyone raised horses to drive and work. In addition to his stud service, Grandpa then milked a few cows, gardened and turned to spending much of his time with his hobby of promoting perpetual motion.

By this time they had built a two-story five-bedroom house with a full basement. It was there that my grandpa began to work with wood to build a contraption for perpetual motion by air and balance. No one was allowed in this area.

Grandpa would allow me to sit on the cellar steps. He often joined me and would tell me of his grandpa and grandma, Peter and Margaret Hardman, who came from Germany after leaving England because of a family disagreement. He also spoke of Civil War experiences and his army friends who also homesteaded in Graham County.

In the early days my grandparents belonged to the Lenora Congregational Church. Later neighbors organized a country Sunday School held at Prairie Dell Country Schoolhouse for many years.

As my grandparents grew older they moved to Lenora to live the rest of their lives. Today the homestead is still owned by the Hardman family.

Irene Hardman Wagoner
Norton, Kansas

Aladdin Lamps and County Fairs

I was born in 1921, and one of my first memories of the farm where I was raised was of the Aladdin lamp my parents had. It made a white light and was such an improvement over the older kerosene lamps. Our neighbors told us they put on their overshoes by the light created by the Aladdin lamp on our back porch when they visited us.

My dad had the first radio in the neighborhood. It ran on batteries. He listened to the first trip Admiral Byrd made to the South Pole and Charles Lindbergh's solo flight to Europe. He and a neighbor listened to prize fights and my mother and the neighbor's wife mended while their men listened to the radio.

At butchering time I helped cut lard into half-inch pieces for rendering and cleaned casings to be used for stuffing sausage and liverwurst. The ham, shoulders and bacon were put into salt brine and then smoked with hickory wood in the smokehouse, as was the sausage. My mother baked our bread and churned our butter and she made her own laundry soap.

Every year we went to the county fair. My mother packed a dinner of fried chicken, potato salad and angel food cake. We ate in our car on the fairground lawn. The entertainment was horse races, displays in the floral hall, livestock shows and milkmaid contests. The merry-go-round, Ferris wheel and pony rides were the biggest attractions on the Midway.

Elaine L. Nebergall

Tipton, Iowa

The Good Kansas Earth

As I reminiscence I often wonder, have I accomplished and achieved my many dreams?

Most of our last three generations were farmers—11 children on Father's side and 12 children on Mother's. In about 1907 my grandfather and an uncle homesteaded in western Kansas near Sharon Springs. There they built a sod house. They were quite creative as it was a two-story sod house, with only a stovepipe to warm the upper story. Years later a small frame house and a wooden windmill were built.

When my parents bought their first Model T Ford touring car all our family visited Grandpa and we saw both houses. There were very few furnishings, no trees and very few fence lines. Most of the surrounding land was pasture land where there had been crop failures; the resulting drifts of dust and sand had grown as high as fence posts. Old sheets were hung over the windows to keep the dust out. Later, when the rains came, they had crops. Irrigation came still later.

Our family of seven children lived west of Junction City. My parents taught us to work with our hands. We always had good things to eat from our huge garden, an orchard, livestock and a dairy herd. There were many problems to solve, as well as much

8

togetherness and fun. School days in rural schools were great. Sometimes there were 32 students, all of whom carried lunches in tin pails. Sandwiches were made of home-baked bread sliced thick. Highlights of the seasons were Christmas, Halloween, Valentine's Day and box suppers. We drove a pony hitched to a cart to school two and a half miles every day.

Father built granaries, barns and sheds as needed. These buildings were demolished and wrecked twice by cyclones and Father had to rebuild. Farm neighbors were the best, so caring and self sacrificing. They created a happy atmosphere for a Christian neighborhood.

With my farm background I married a neighboring farmer. This indeed was one of the highlights of my life. We wanted to own some farm acreage. After renting and sharing during the Depression we were able to make a small payment on a farm. It was an ideal stock farm with a big new two-story house, a basement and a barn. A spring-fed creek nearby was of great value to the livestock, as the water temperature remained consistent during all four seasons.

Our love for livestock combined with careful management soon yielded a huge herd of cattle, so we bought an adjoining pasture with a pond. With a large flock of laying hens and many litters of baby pigs each season, we reaped many rewards.

Along with going to our country church, we enjoyed our farm life so much our work became our pleasure. After church we shared Sunday dinners with friends.

Due to my husband's health problems we were forced to leave the farm of happy memories. We moved into town where I had been previously employed for five years. Since my husband's passing and my retirement I have returned to my lifelong hobby of writing poems and stories.

I feel very fortunate to have experienced this Kansas home-spun love of the land among friends and many relatives.

Grace Britt Horner

Junction City, Kansas

Happy Hollow Farm

Some people don't like to think about their poor upbringing or the hard times. Maybe I'm crazy, but I love to think about those days. In my mind I go back there, and it gives me a good feeling. Though my mother and dad have been gone for many years now, I get homesick to go back there. It was in a deep hollow where eight of us kids grew up, in a little shack of a house, just a little rocky farm with a beautiful spring flowing in our backyard. We used the cave that the spring flowed from as a cellar. We had cement shelves in there to set canned jars of fruit and vegetables on, because they would not freeze in the winter and in the summer they would stay nice and cool. In the winter, when the air was cold, you could see the steam coming out as the air from the cave hit the cold air outside.

That cave served a lot of purposes. We kids would go back in there and get clay to mold things out of to play with. We would go exploring with neighboring young folks, who would bring flashlights and lanterns and see how far they could go. The cave narrowed down and they could never get too far, but it was fun. Neighbor boys would play with my brothers and have big water fights around the spring—there was no shortage of water. On hot days when Dad was gone and we were playing our games, Mother would take a quilt and lay it in the cave where it was nice and cool and read her only book, *The Shepherd of the Hills*. She loved that story so much; she would lay in there and read it and cry. How she would enjoy the play they now put on taken from that story.

We had a few milk cows that we all helped with. My sister, Roma, and I nearly always had to go hunt them and drive them in, but we enjoyed our trip. Along the way we would find things to see and do, such as pick wild flowers or grapes. There was an old leaning tree we always tried to push over. We always thought it was about to fall but it never did. Standing on one hill we would listen for the cowbell and hear it in the distance, so down into the hollow we would go and up the next hill.

There was always night wood to carry in, that was a never-ending chore. We had a wood cookstove, so that required wood year-round too. Dad farmed the fields, and my older brothers helped him. Mother helped in the fields till the boys got big enough, then she stayed at the house with the ever-present little ones.

She would have dinner cooked for the ones who went to work. It was a busy place. It makes me sad to go there now, it's so quiet. When I go I always have to call for Mother, for she was always there, and it makes me cry. I listen to the brook that trickles along in front of the house so peacefully. Some of the most exciting times we had there were when it rained a lot and the creek rose. It nearly always happened at night and we would all peer out the windows waiting for a flash of lightning so we could see. We had no big floodlight to turn on. Our little peaceful brook would be leaping and lunging, our yard was built up and high above the branch bed and we had a foot bridge that lay across it. The water would be up even with the edge of the yard, then someone would yell, "Out went the foot log." It was kind of scary. We always thought we were going to get washed away, but we never did. The rain would slacken and the high water would go down a little so we could all go to bed and rest in peace. The next morning the sun would shine on the hills and rocks washed clean from the rain. Our little stream was quite peaceful again and the excitement was all over till the next spring.

My dad always had some pretty horses. He would trim his bridles and harness with pretty tassels and buckles. He plowed the fields and worked hard to make a living on that little farm. We kept some hogs to butcher, chickens to lay eggs, and we always raised a big garden. We depended on that for food. After a hard winter with no fresh vegetables that garden stuff was a welcome sight to us. We enjoyed those good summer dinners of new potatoes, cabbage, green beans, onions and wilted lettuce. I'll never forget how good it was. My folks had a hard time raising us but they stayed together and did their best. I love them and honor them for it. I'm so thankful for that little rocky farm in the hills.

Zoe Davis Bilyeu
Forsyth, Missouri

We Thrived on Fresh Air and Freedom

There were six of us, four boys and two girls. We were born and raised in a small town in Pennsylvania. As the older children were getting on toward their teenage years, my father decided to buy a farm and move us there, as he thought the city might not be the best environment for us to grow up in. The farm had a house, a barn, a chicken coop and everything else a typical farm has. We liked it and thrived on the fresh air and freedom. Beside the six of us kids, our great-uncle lived with us, so that made nine that Mom had to cook and wash for and tend to.

I can't remember any of us ever being hungry. My dad hunted and fished. Mom disliked game and fish but she could cook it really great. Mom baked nine loaves of bread every other day, as well as cinnamon rolls. There is nothing like coming home from school and smelling that special odor and tasting those delicious rolls. We also had lots of homemade soup—not just a pan of it, but a huge pot cooked on the wood stove.

On this farm we had chickens, a couple of cows, a pony and some pigs. Dad wasn't home so the animals gave the six of us something to do. My four brothers were something else. One day they were in the woods and came home with three young skunks—where the mother was I don't remember—but the skunks needed a mother, so we put them in with some kittens that were just born, and low and behold the mother cat took them like they were her own, nursing them and caring for them. Some of you won't believe this, but we also had an old setting hen who needed to do some mothering, so when the cat got off the nest, the hen got on and thought she had chicks under her. The *Erie Daily News* came one day and took pictures of the skunks in the nest, and had a little write-up in the paper about the strange doings on our farm.

We didn't have a swimming pool, but it doesn't take kids long to find out that swimming in the creek will suffice just fine when it is hot and humid. Besides, swimming there probably saved us getting the galvanized tub out and heating the water to take a bath.

Our life on the farm taught us to get along together and

showed us that we could do without a lot of fancy things in life. We all came out the better for our experiences and the love that our parents gave us.

Audrey Lavery
Meadville, Pennsylvania

The Old Stepping Stone

Though age has dimmed my eyesight and slowed my step, when I was looking at the cedar trees and cement walks around my childhood home, I was astonished to see the old six-foot sturdy rock that made the stepping stone to our front porch in the same place and apparently as sturdy as I remembered.

In 1910, my family and I moved from our family farm that we all loved to a comfortable home in a small town. We had to move to a smaller home because of the early death of my father and an accident that crippled my grandfather.

Twenty-two years later when my brother was grown, he married, and with his competent and understanding wife took the old grandparents back to the farm home to enjoy their later years. Inquiring further I learned that the first house where the old rock was placed had burned in 1949. Another house much like the old one was moved in and placed so that the cement walks and the old rock were never moved. For 49 years this house was home to the family who made these changes.

When outdoor carpet became popular the porch and the old rock were covered. Therefore, it wasn't noticed until the house was sold for storage to an adjoining school.

Now at 90 I ask myself, should I try to buy the old stone? Should I try to have it moved to my present home? Would it crumble? Should I leave the old stepping stone where it was placed by someone long ago to be used and enjoyed by generations?

Bonnie Dunlap
Montrose, Missouri

Homespun Entertainment was Best

My Grandfather Wartig came to the United States in the early 1900s and moved to Missouri with his wife and five children around 1910. He was a dignified and reserved man with a thick accent that made it difficult to understand him at times. He took the train to look for land, and upon returning home from one of these trips, he told his family that he had met a man on the train who "tried to pump me. But," he added triumphantly, "I didn't have my handle out."

Grandfather believed in getting all he could out of his tax dollars, and since he owned land in two school districts, he sent his two youngest girls to another school district for two months of the year, while their regular school was not in session.

My dad bought the family farm and raised his two children there. They built Highway 36 through our town in the 1920s. Upon its completion, Dad bought one of the two roadhouses that had been used to house the workers. It was equipped with two full-size bunk beds with storage drawers beneath them, a long mess table with benches, a claw-footed bathtub, a wood cookstove and many cupboards. Dad used it for his hired man and wife, later removing the trucks it was setting on and putting it on a permanent foundation. I remember how my dad and this hired man would make many trips, each carrying two five-gallon buckets of water to our truck patch after supper to save our food supply from the drought. The trucks were used by many neighbors and acquaintances for moving buildings.

Dad and a neighbor then used the roadhouse to build crystal sets and radios. The neighbor had children the same age as my brother and me, so we looked forward to the evenings after the chores were done when we could get together with our friends.

After the men had finished with their radio work, they would often come into the house and play Rook. We children would go to the kitchen, make a batch of fudge and pop some popcorn. The fudge went to sugar more often than not, but I don't remember hearing anyone complain.

With a theater six and a half miles away that showed three different movies per week, we didn't have to travel far for adequate entertainment. We probably enjoyed the homespun versions of entertainment best, however, such as the mandatory programs that the rural schools had to give four times a year in addition to the last day of school program. We often went to the programs put on by children in adjoining districts as well.

The women had extension clubs where they learned the latest trends in homemaking, such as caning chairs, upholstery, landscaping, using pressure cookers for canning and some delicious new recipes that often contained heavy, rich cream. The Ladies Aid of the rural church met monthly, having all-day meetings during the winter months when the men were invited to come for dinner. The church's young adult class had parties every month at various homes. All the children were welcome at these parties, where the babies went to sleep and were laid on beds atop the visitors' coats.

The country church furnished entertainment with its various programs, family basket dinners and potluck suppers. At a revival meeting held there once, some men came from Kentucky and played their saws. It was fascinating to me as well as melodious and beautiful.

School wasn't called off because of snow in the winters. When it was actually as high as the tops of the fences and crusty enough to support considerable weight, my brother and I would hitch our Shetland pony to our large Red Flyer sled. We'd go down the road where we picked up two more sleds and be off to school on top of the drifted snow. We were at the north end of the district and I suppose the snowplow just didn't get to us, because the road south of the school, where most of the pupils and the teacher lived, would be open days before ours was.

As soon as I could reach the pedals, I drove the Model T Ford truck down the rows of the cornfield while Dad and my brother shucked a temporary supply that would last until they took the team and wagon and worked at it all day.

Most of the farmers had their own road drags and maintained the dirt roads. I would get to ride with my feet dragging off the back, which meant getting home covered with dust and having to get into the bathtub.

Perhaps I am so earthy today because it seems I enjoyed riding in low vehicles during my childhood. The bobsled was another favorite form of transportation for me. My maternal grandparents lived six miles north of us and we would often visit them covered with lap robes and woolen army blankets. I don't ever remember arriving cold.

Jo Buddenberg
Hamilton, Missouri

Wings Over the Plains

Living 79 years in Buffalo County, Nebraska, has been a glorious adventure, and it continues to be a joyful and heartwarming life with highs and lows. I was a rural schoolteacher when Rudolf began courting me. Two years later, in May 1936, we married. This ended my career, as the rule was no married teachers. We gave our children wings and Christian training, and if I could do it over, I'd teach them all to dance!

We rented this homestead place of my father's with its two quarters of land, so when a salesman came up to my school north of Amherst with a piano on a trailer, I got it for $75 and rode with him to our farm where he and Rudy unloaded it—I have it yet today, 59 years later.

My father-in-law gave each of his seven children $1000 when they married. My, that came in handy to buy four horses, a wagon, a car, a new kitchen range, a table, chairs, bed and dresser and a couple of pieces of used machinery. Rudy had been farming with his dad and had learned all the best ways to sow and harvest and manage horses, cattle and hog chores. He had planted a field of wheat in the fall, borrowing machinery from my father as his home was 13 miles north.

Rudy picked me up every Thursday night at my boarding place to join three of his cousins and their wives in a catechism class. I was confirmed in the Lutheran faith in April in St. Paul's Church seven miles north of Riverdale. It was only three and a half miles from our farm. It was such a blessing to begin our married life with a church home and to be a part of a Bible class group that had a social once a month.

Rudy's sisters decorated that country church for our wedding on May 24, 1936. Another couple was married the following Sunday evening while the streamers were still in place. Mother had a reception for friends and relatives. I wore a long, white dress from the Sears and Roebuck catalog. My sister-in-law let me use her veil and silk flowers.

Rudy played baseball with a team that had uniforms, and I learned to really like going to the games. He also played guitar and sang at weddings and funerals. Fishing, hunting and fixing-up machinery were his talents. My dad was so glad to have help with repairs and building fences and windmills.

We did not have a honeymoon. Rudy got some hens from home so we had fresh eggs, and we started milking a couple of cows and planted a garden. Father trucked in apples and pears from Iowa, and I got 45 quarts of fruit to put in the cellar under the house.

When we had been married eight years, Rudy had a heart attack cranking up silage and was flat on his back for two weeks. The doctor said if he'd take it easy for a year he'd be able to do things again, and he did mend in a year. My older brother, Harold, was just back from the army, and he helped carry on the farming that year. We hired neighbor boys to scoop cobs and other jobs.

Father was killed in a car accident in 1952. We bought this homestead place in the settlement of the estate and began looking for a schoolhouse or a house to replace the old house we had used for 18 years. It had been a halfway house between Broken Bow and Kearney during those early years when Grandpa Ferdinand Juhl lived there and let pioneers water their horses and stay overnight.

We found a lovely two-story house that we could buy in 1954, one and a half miles to the west as the crow flies. The lady even came down on the price. I made out the check for $4500, as they were anxious to get their affairs in order and leave for Washington state to be near a son. Rudy had a basement dug, and now we had a bathroom and water in the house.

Rudy and the boys changed every building on this homestead place save the old granary the tornado wrecked in 1993. The windbreaks he planted years ago proved to be blessings. We bought an adjoining quarter of land and had more pasture. When the St. Paul's congregation disbanded, Rudy bought the church and remodeled it as our barn and had a milking parlor installed to use for several years. The equipment came from a nephew's sale. We celebrated our 25th and 40th anniversaries with open houses at the church followed by suppers for relatives.

After Rudy died on our 41st anniversary, I painted all the outside buildings two coats that summer in a special effort. The oldest son had come home five years earlier to help with the farming. He does such a good job managing the 480 acres and keeping up with chores, fences and repairs.

The oldest son put down a pivot 10 years ago after all our former years of dryland farming. The buildings sit in the middle of a section, so our electric power comes in a half-mile from the east, and our driveway is a half-mile from the south. The telephone line is underground.

We owe those early surveyors a vote of thanks for marking out sections of lands and areas for roads. Rudy served on Divide township church and school boards. He is buried in the Riverdale Cemetery. He was the captain of our ship for many years! Thank you, Lord, for all the help.

Dorothy Carmann
Riverdale, Nebraska

The Air was Fresh and Life was Good

My parents homesteaded on a 640-acre farm 17 miles northeast of Kiowa, Colorado. My father was a mail carrier for a small post office and store called Hargisville, which my Grandfather Hargis

Hargis owned. In 1913 there was a terrible blizzard and my father could drive the horses and sled right over the tops of fences afterward, as the snow was so deep and packed hard. Winters were sometimes pretty rough but the summers were beautiful.

There wasn't much entertainment then—just the programs we put on at school. When I was six the neighbors around the county began having house parties about every weekend, and we would go and dance until the wee hours of the morning. Our music was someone with a fiddle or a phonograph.

I think it was around 1927 when we finally got a radio that ran on batteries, which was used very frugally.

In the summertime there would usually be a Fourth of July picnic. It featured horse races, ball games, sack races, egg-and-spoon contests, and whatever else anyone could think of for fun. These picnics were usually held in a large clearing near some trees, so we would have shade to set up picnic tables.

We went to church pretty regularly in spite of the fact that we had to drive a horse and buggy about 10 miles one way. We would even go to revival meetings at night when the only light to guide us was a kerosene lantern or the moon!

The younger generation of today would probably think we had a very dull life, but we were very happy in those days and much healthier as we breathed pure fresh air.

Esther Tweden
Commerce City, Colorado

Ancestors Chose Their Land Well

I still live less than a quarter of a mile from the house on the family farm where I was born 80 years ago! Not too many folks are able to do that in these years of people on the move. The farm is in southeastern Iowa, 45 minutes south of Iowa City, where the University of Iowa is located. Our place is a "Century Farm" and then some. I have my great-grandfather's diary about buying land and moving here from Illinois in the 1860s.

The family got here a few years before the railroad got beyond the county seat town. In the early days many people homesteaded close to rivers to be sure of water and trees for fuel and lumber. My ancestor, Theophilus, hired a wagon on his first visit and drove a half day from the end of the rails. He chose some of the flattest, blackest ground in this part of the state. A family from nearer the river moved up on the prairie too, and in a few years my grandfather married their older daughter. That family and descendants still live on the other side of the section from ours.

One of my most vivid memories goes back to before I was married. I have a sister four and a half years younger than I am. In 1924 there was a terrible storm the night of my birthday, June 29. Our mother was frantically trying to mop up rain coming in broken windows after a severe hailstorm. She parked us on the spare bed downstairs and said not to move. Every so often she would come in with a flashlight, pointing it in our faces, to see if we were still safe and dry. There was no electricity. Almost every window on one side of the house had broken. I was mad about the light in my face and my sister was crying bitterly. What a night!

When she married, my sister moved more than 50 miles away. I still live where I can see that farmhouse. It has been cared for and lived in by the farmer who has operated it for many years.

Helen K. Stoutner
Keota, Iowa

Smart Horses Stepped Over the Baby

When my husband, Corwin, was 18 months old, his mother asked his older sisters to take him outdoors to play while she prepared supper. The children went to play by the open barn door. There was a step in front of the door and the girls had their little brother sit on the step so they could keep an eye on him. Father came home from the fields with the work horses. He unhitched the horses in the yard as was his custom. The horses would race each other into the barn to see who would be the first at the feed trough.

The horses took off at full gallop. The girls saw the horses running toward them and ran out of the way, leaving their baby brother sitting on the step. Both of the horses stopped in front of the baby, stepped ever so gently over him and then continued their race through the barn to the feed box. Father saw all of this, but it happened so fast he was powerless to do anything. Years later he said he thought he was going to have a heart attack.

My husband came from a large farm family. There were two boys and six girls. Money was not very plentiful in the growing up years. Each year they would raise three acres of sugar beets, which the children helped harvest. The money was used to buy school clothes and new shoes. Each fall the boys received one new pair of overalls and two flannel shirts. One year the boys were so proud of their clothes, they asked Mother if they could wear them on the Sunday afternoon before school started. Mother said yes, but not to play by the creek because she didn't want them to get their new clothes dirty. One side of the barn roof sloped to within three feet of the ground. The boys thought it would be great fun to slide down the roof. After an afternoon of sliding they went into the house only to discover they had worn out the seat of their new overalls. There wasn't money for another new pair, so they wore "fanny patches" on their jeans for the whole school year. Nowadays they might be in style, but it sure hurt their pride back then.

During the slow time on the farm, Father would take a job with the sugar beet factory. He would always buy a year's supply of sugar for the family and store it in the attic. The year rationing started during World War II, they already had their supply. Mother didn't know what to do. The children were told not to tell anyone about the sugar in the attic. They were not allowed to play in the attic when they had friends over either. Was Mother ever glad when the next canning season arrived and she could use up a large portion of the sugar horde.

Sylvia Van Den Bosch
Holland, Michigan

Moving to Missouri

It was March 1931 when Mom went to the hospital. I was play-ing in front of our house when a big truck stopped. Mama was in the front seat holding a baby wrapped in blankets. Mama got out of the truck and said, "This is your new brother." George and I named him William Charles Smith; William after his dad, William Henry Smith, and Charles after his Uncle Charlie, William Henry's brother.

We stayed there on Eighth Street until school was out, because Dad had sold the house on Sixth Street and the people wanted to move right in. Now that school was out Mom and Dad were getting things ready to move.

Daddy hired a big truck to move us. Mama's brother, Uncle John, was to drive it to Pierce City, Missouri. All the furniture was loaded on along with all of our belongings. The mattresses were loaded last, tied down good so they would hold the furniture on and not blow off. The loaded truck was parked by the house, ready to get an early start the next day. We all stayed at the McClures that night. They were Dad's kin through marriage, and they lived in back of us on Seventh Street. After loading the truck, it rained real hard all night, soaking things on the truck good.

Sometime around noon we got to the farm. I don't remember the person who drove us to Pierce City or the way we got there. I do remember the rocky road we were on and Mama saying there is your new home up there by that big oak tree.

There it was, a two-story farmhouse, a log wood shed by itself and a chicken house, a corn crib and a cow barn all together. There was a cherry orchard to the west, a strawberry patch on the east end and a grape patch on the north side of the acreage—all on 20 acres.

There was no water on the property except for the pond. There was a cistern but no water in it. Grandpa had put a cover over the hole where rain water was suppose to flow in. The rain troughs around the house drained water into the cistern. There was a well pump on top of this cistern. There was also an outhouse set off from the barn by itself.

There were no electric lights on the farm; we used kerosene lamps. In Pittsburg, Kansas, we had electric lights and cold running water. There was a wood stove in the kitchen where Mom did all of her cooking and heating up. There was a big iron stove in the front room to help heat up the house and the upstairs. There was one bedroom downstairs; we kids had to sleep in the open upstairs. There were no partitions to separate us from Luella, we all slept in two beds; Luella and Reuben in one and Raymond and me in the other.

It was two miles to town, and the only way we got there was to walk. Later Dad bought a wagon and buggy. Dad kept the buggy and wagon parked on the east end of the barn. The buggy did not have a top on it, so when it rained the leather got wet then had to dry out. All the time it sat out in the weather the leather stayed soft and never did crack or dry out.

When Dad got the wagon we hauled water from the Tarpey Farm in barrels and put this water in the cistern. One cold, drizzly day Dad and I had to haul water. It was cold and miserable but we got water hauled to the cistern. When it rained we would catch rain water from the house, which flowed into the cistern—then we no longer needed to haul water.

> George H. Smith
> Muskogee, Oklahoma

Searching for a Permanent Home

When New Mexico opened for homesteading, my father rode his bicycle 400 miles from his father's homestead in Oklahoma to New Mexico. He filed his claim on 160 acres of government land near the little settlement of Roy, New Mexico.

When my father and mother were married in 1913, their possessions consisted of a snug one-room claim shack on that 160 acres and the bicycle with father's photography equipment strapped on the back.

Everything went well for my parents during those early years. Their acreage doubled, the house grew to three large rooms with porches, a small photograph shop was opened in town and the farming equipment increased along with the horses and cattle. The children came along to help with the chores. I was the third child, and I can remember gathering eggs and helping to pull young tumbleweeds out of the garden.

Then came what my father called "the prosperous years." During that time my father's crops expanded until he was raising 100 acres of pinto beans and 100 acres of wheat each for several years. It was like the Bible reference to seven years of plenty followed by seven years of drought and famine. By 1928 the well-known "dust bowl days" had started. In New Mexico there were terrible sandstorms. During the early summer, my father was able to buy a wrecked Greyhound Bus. The motor was good, but the body was badly damaged. That bus became my father's obsession; he worked to make it into a comfortable motor home to take his family out of New Mexico to the "promised land," the Ozarks. Every spare minute of daylight was spent working on that bus. Every night was spent under the coal oil lamp, poring over United Farms and Strout's Catalog of Ozark farms. He marked all of the farms listed that he wanted to see. He told us that there were trees with cool shade in the Ozarks, brooks with cool running water and rivers that had nice big fish just waiting to be caught and eaten. There were wild berries to pick and rich ground to raise good gardens. Best of all there would be no blowing sand.

One memorable evening my father came home from town in a very happy mood. That night at the supper table he pulled out a crisp, new $100 bill. He passed it around the table and let each one of us feel and handle it; he told us that it was the down-payment on our farm in the Ozarks. I never thought to ask, but I think that was money saved back a small amount at a time over a long period, until that day when it reached the amount to take to the bank.

During the school term of 1928-29 the sandstorms were extremely bad. Several of our neighbors just gave up and moved out, going to California. Crops were poor that fall because of no rain, and we had to make good use of everything we had raised in the garden. Our pumpkins turned out to be our best crop, so Mama canned a lot of pumpkin butter and tomato preserves for winter sweetness for our bread. I can remember thinking I had a real good school lunch when I opened my half-gallon syrup bucket at noon and found two muffins, split and spread with pumpkin butter.

The most unforgettable part of that last school term was our walks home from school against that furiously blowing sand. Day after day, Bonnie and I would make that one and one-half mile fight against that vicious, cutting sand. At times there would seem to be a lull in its fierceness; at that time we would run as fast and as far as we could, knowing that after the lull it would come on more fierce than before. During the storm's fury, we would squat down in the road and wrap our dresses around our burning legs and hide our faces and arms against our knees, staying quietly in that position until another lull seemed to come. We would come home crying, with our arms and legs and faces as red as the worst sunburn and just as painful. Mama would bring out a little bowl of fresh sweet cream and gently pat it all over our pain to soothe it. If it was baking day, we got half a buttered hot roll apiece, and if Papa was in the house he would remind us if we could only endure it until school was out, we would be leaving New Mexico forever.

Finally the last days of school came. Mama and Papa worked hard to have everything ready. What a wonderful, ingenious father we had! He thought of every detail to make that bus a complete summer home for our family. There was a bunk for every kid—according to his size—and a storage compartment under the bunks for keeping each child's clothes, bedding and treasures. There was a full-size bed across the back, and just inside the door was the washstand, with frames built to hold the washpan and the water bucket so they would not spill when traveling over the roughest roads. The outside had some handy features too. The cupboard was built outside, next to the door; shelves held the dishes, silverware and staples, with the pots and pans below. The door of the cupboard was hinged to the bottom of the box, with a secure latch at the top and a sturdy leg hinged to the center, so that when the cupboard was opened, the door became our table. A platform across the back of the bus held the "putt-putt" gasoline-engine washing machine with two black washtubs, a boiler, a big canning kettle and campfire equipment. A good length of clothes-line wire was coiled neatly along the back of bus, and there was even a neat doghouse built on the back of the fender for Snip and her puppies. We also had a tent for inclement weather. When we got home from the last day of school, everything was ready for us to leave the next morning.

So this was the day we had waited for so long! We were migrants, venturing on to an unknown road. We left that morning—our parents, six children, a mother dog and her three puppies—on the day after school was out in 1929. We left one brother buried in New Mexico. This was a cherished, memorable summer, the high-light of my entire life. I would be 11 on my birthday in June.

We arrived in Missouri just two days later. Our timing was right, for the strawberry picking season was just starting. We were paid 2 cents a quart, and we picked berries for several growers as long as the season lasted. All of us children were good workers, as we had been taught to work and enjoyed working, but it soon became apparent that our brother John was an excellent straw-berry picker. He could keep up with the other Missouri boys who had been picking for several years.

Mama liked to pick strawberries. She would generally pick one carrierful to start the morning, then she would take her place in the packing shed, where she could keep Baby Martha, who was less than 1 year old, with her. She would bring the culled berries home with her and make strawberry jam at night.

Every Friday evening we looked for a clear running brook where we could camp for the weekend. Saturday was washing day for our family. After breakfast Saturday morning we all carried water—heated over the campfire—to the black tub. The putt-putt washer was set down off the platform, and the rinse tub sat on the platform under the wringer. The clothesline was stretched to a tree and we were in business. Sometimes a pot of beans cooked on the campfire beside the boiler. If possible, Papa and John would try to find a fishing hole within walking distance so we might have a mess of fish for supper. We would all have a bath before we went to bed, either in the creek or the rinse tub. We knew what clean clothes we would put on in the morning, because every Sunday morning we would go to the nearest little country church for worship. It really didn't matter too much what denomination it was.

One day we stopped at a gas station. We children ran out back of the station—where the toilets were located in those days—then back to the bus, ready to go again. We had gone about 10 miles when we came to an intersection. My father, unsure of which road to take, pulled over to look at his map. While we were stopped an old pickup pulled alongside and asked, "Are you all a missin' a little bit of a tiny girl and a little yaller shepherd dog? Well, she's back at that fillin' station." We looked around and sure enough, our 4-and-a-half-year-old, Dollie, was missing. Of course we turned right around and quickly headed back to the station. I was the one who was admonished. Papa said, "Since you are the oldest girl, you should check that everyone gets back on the bus when we stop like that." When we got back to the station, there was Dollie, sitting on the corner of the gas pump with her arm around the dog. She was not crying. When she saw us she stood up and smiled sweetly and said, "I told Snippy not to worry, 'cause you would come back and get us." The man at the station then told Papa that a neighbor there was wanting to hire someone to paint his barn. He gave directions and we drove to the place, where we set up camp in their backyard. We were there about a week, for it was a big barn for Papa and John to paint. The whole family was busy that week—there were several summer apple trees, with the ground under them literally covered with fallen apples. The lady of the house told Mama we could have as many as we wanted; she had been working on them but there were more than they could possibly use. Mama made the best applesauce out of them. We girls picked up apples by the bucketfuls, and Mama canned 24 quarts of applesauce.

We found and visited all of the farms that my father had marked in his Ozark Farm Catalogs, but most of them had drawbacks. They were either too far away from a town with a good high school, or the road leading to them was so bad we would be isolated in winter weather. We finally found our "perfect Ozark farm" on a hill, just one and a half miles from Neosho. We had close neighbors, and we all spent many happy days working and playing together on that wonderful farm. We were right in the heart of berry country, where we enjoyed a simple but pleasurable country life. We children graduated from Neosho High School, married Camp Crowder soldiers, and scattered after World War II, but we have always considered Neosho our home. Our parents and baby brother are buried there, as is one fun-loving sister who we can never forget.

No matter how old we get or how far we roam, nothing can erase the memory of that glorious summer of 1929 when our family went searching for another permanent farm home.

Mellie Coones
Warsaw, Missouri

———■———

Chapter 2: Fun on the Farm

The Taffy Pull

When I was a child, farm people had less work in the winter months than during the growing season. We had a little more time for parties! The Saturday evening before Valentine's Day grew to become a neighborhood taffy pull. Everybody planned on it for weeks ahead. In our family it was an important event. We did all the little things that could be done in advance. For example: every one of us had his new pair of hand-knit, long, black woolen stockings finished and ready for the party. This was an activity that the whole family participated in after the evening dishes were done. Santa brought Virginia knitting needles when she was 2 years old!

The day of the party found all of us up and busy. The weather was very cold and the sky was clear. That evening we milked the 13 cows early. Agnes, my eldest sister, had the food ready to put on the table when we brought the cream in. We sat right down and ate. Agnes washed the dishes; I put them away. Mother got Virginia ready. Father went out to the barn, lifted the harnesses off their pegs and put them on the horses. He got down the strings of bells, placed them over the horses' shoulders, and secured them safely with a girth just behind their forelegs. He hitched the team to the sled. The last thing he did was to fill the sled box full of nice, fresh yellow straw and cover it with a big, dry blanket.

While Father was getting the horses and the sled ready we put on our clean long underwear, the black knitted socks, our petticoats and our very best dresses. I had button shoes; Agnes had slippers! I wished I had slippers, too. Mother called, "Girls, don't forget your muffs, scarves and stocking caps." She walked over to the organ, picked up Father's violin and placed it on the table beside the picnic basket. She said, "We must not forget the violin." The faint tinkle of bells grew louder and louder. Mother called, "Father is ready!" We hastily put on our coats. Mother handed each of us a huge, hot block of wood that she had been heating in the oven. She wrapped them and the only hot soapstone we owned in old blankets. She cautioned us saying, "These are extremely hot! Don't burn yourselves! Agnes, will you carry the soapstone for Virginia? Lucille, can you help Virginia get into the sleigh? I have our passing dishes in the picnic basket. I want to check the fireplace. I will bring the basket and the violin."

Father laughed when he looked at us. He said, "You girls look like miniature ladies carrying newborn babies wrapped in receiving blankets!" We sat down on the blanket. It was fun to feel the soft, fluffy straw settle down beneath us. We placed the warm sticks and soapstone under our feet and wrapped the long scarves over our heads and necks. We poked our hands into our woolly muffs. Father threw another big blanket over all of us. He asked, "Everybody cozy and snug?" Holding the reins in one hand he slapped them gently across the horses' rumps and sang out, "Giddy up, Fred! Giddy up, Bill!" We were off.

The stars blinked at us. We looked for the Big Dipper and the Little Dipper. We imagined the Big Bear and the Little Bear. Before we knew it we could see the twinkle of the farmhouse lights where we were headed. The kerosene lights in all the windows got brighter and brighter. Father drove right up to the back door. He called out, "Whoa! Whoa!"

Mrs. White hustled us in saying, "Step lively, girls! We don't need Jack Frost or any of his children inside. Go right on in and shut the door." Activity was going on everywhere. Big girls were directing big young men to move furniture to their rooms. Other men were down on the floor rolling back the carpet. The whole room was soon empty except for the organ and a couple of chairs. Father came in with his violin. Rosie sat down at the organ and gave him an "A" tone. He tuned his violin and began with "Turkey in the Straw!" Uncle Jim stood on a low stool and began calling. The floor filled with eager dancers. Father played one tune after another: "Girl I Left Behind Me," "Old Zip Coon," "Four Hands Around," "Virginia Reel," "Arkansas Traveler" and more. When one girl wanted to dance, another stepped up to the organ and played the chords.

Occasionally somebody called out for a waltz or a two-step. My father handed the violin to me and said, "I want Agnes to dance with me." I played "The Last Rose of Summer."(I was only 7 and it was the only song slow enough for me to play.) Then he danced the schottische with me. He absolutely loved dancing the schottische! He was tall and danced beautifully! Nobody else came out so we had the whole floor. I was so happy and so proud!

Just then the ladies in the kitchen rang the cow bell. Somebody called out, "The taffy is ready!" One lady had chunks of soft taffy just right for pulling. She came into the living room and distributed it among the former dancers and spectators. I wandered into the kitchen. Mother had a pan of clean snow into which other cooks dropped strings of stringy, glistening golden syrup. Mother knew when it was ready to be removed from the wood-burning range. Soon all the cooks had finished boiling it and it was cool enough to divide. To this day, I can see the long strings of candy we pulled back and forth again and again. I can also see some of those cables and cords stretching thinner and thinner until several broke in the center and slid gracefully, still glistening, upon the bare floor! Nobody thought that a major calamity. They just gathered it up, formed a ball and started pulling again! The whole room was full of the sweet, vanilla aroma. Suddenly a mystery happened. The stringy stuff changed color and began to harden. We hastily pulled it into one last, long slender string and let it cool. It was ready to eat!

Between two and three we picked our coats out of a pile two feet high and put them on. Mother bundled Virginia, who had fallen asleep with the other infants, and carried her outdoors and into our sleigh. I was thinking I was glad I was old enough to have stayed awake. With our taffy in a little bag, Father covered us quickly. As we rode out of the White's yard their lights went out. I remember asking, "Mother, what did you all put in that taffy?"

I heard her say, "Two cups of sugar, a two-pound can of Karo Syrup, one cup of vinegar, a pinch of salt..."

Suddenly, Father was shaking my shoulder. He shook me long enough and hard enough so that I staggered into our house, still clutching my bag of inch-long lengths of white taffy. I found my bed; I fell down on it. The next morning I was still holding my candy.

Lucille Stanek Jenkins
Jackson, Michigan

The Run of the Farm

My widowed mother rented a farmhouse for a couple of years when I was 8 and 9. Of her 14 kids, five of us were under 16 and there were usually two or three nieces and nephews visiting. We pretty much had the run of the farm, so we had lots of things to do. We played in the barn loft, made a room of hay bales, walked the rafters and regularly visited the pigeon roost. Once I went in the roost and found a big black snake in a nest. I got out of there fast! A day or two later, Mom found a big black snake in a duck's nest and killed it. It had swallowed a duck egg. We thought it was the same one I had seen, or at least we hoped so.

We had a playhouse in a patch of horse weeds. It was a great place to play and we didn't know it was hot!

We played in the creek and pond and slid on the ice in winter. My sister fell through once where the cattle water hole was, but it was shallow and she got right out and high-tailed it to the house.

My favorite place was the top of a mulberry tree, where I would read or sing. It had a divided trunk, and I was the only one who could climb it. I read everything I could lay my hands on, including "True Story" and "True Confessions" that belonged to my older sisters.

Jane Shepard Dungy
Stewartsville, Missouri

Saturday Night House Dances

We had no TV for entertainment back in the '20s and '30s. We had to find things to do for recreation. The farm folks in our neighborhood took turns having dances at each others' houses on Saturday nights. When it was our turn, I remember how we moved furniture out of the way, rolled up the rugs in a couple of rooms, and sprinkled corn meal on the bare wood floors to make them nice and smooth to dance on. My mother's uncle played the fiddle and our neighbor was the square dance caller. I can still hear him calling, "A dosie-do on the corners all, around your honey with a little more do, and promenade all. You know where and I don't care."

About 11:30 I would help my mother serve sandwiches and coffee. This was followed by a few waltzes or fox-trots and then "Home, Sweet Home." A good time was had by all.

In the winter, our heating stoves complicated matters, so we'd have a card party instead. Everyone enjoyed playing Pedro, which was followed by a light lunch near midnight. The folks left for home soon after, for the farmers had to get up early the next morning to do the milking and other chores.

Marie Wyatt
Elyria, Ohio

A Proud Rural Heritage

I wouldn't take a million for my childhood farm experiences. All that fun, the work ethic, the home-grown food and the time for meditation and dreams. What an opportunity for character building!

We tested our imaginations as we played on tire swings or roller-skated on ground hard packed by cloudbursts or hail. We climbed trees and sheds and haymows; we jumped down into wheat bins; we built nests in straw piles. We looked for bird feathers and wild flowers, the first ripe fruit, or fresh vegetables to pull.

In winter, games were the things to enjoy. Sometimes uncles stayed with us to help harvest corn. They gave us competition at

Monopoly, dominoes, checkers and various card games. As she baked bread or crocheted, Mother laughed along with the rest of us.

My older sister and I dressed paper dolls for hours. Sometimes we cut models from catalogs and created fashions for them. Shoe boxes were decorated for rooms, and matchboxes held their clothes. As farm children we were capable of entertaining ourselves.

We owned cars, but if they didn't start, or if the dirt roads were impassable, we were hauled to school in the grain wagon, pulled by a team of faithful horses. Neighbor children were picked up on the way. The bottom of the wagon was covered with straw. Mother provided quilts for warmth. Dad sang songs such as "Tiptoe Through the Tulips." These were fun times.

Farming wasn't all fun and games. There were frantic dashes to the cellar when a tornado was sighted. Droughts kept the grain bins empty, and the animals subsequently suffered from a lack of food. At times the heat would be almost too much to bear. Grasshoppers ate everything in sight. Cloudbursts washed out the corn. Somehow we farmers always found the strength to start anew, helping each other through all types of emergencies, including the time our coal shed caught fire. Neighbors gathered and poured buckets of water on the fire to save the shed. Claire and I watched from a tree branch where we were picking mulberries for supper.

Sometimes, when I'm in a dreamy or melancholy mood, I get flashbacks of childhood happenings: finding a nest of pheasant eggs; sneaking May baskets to a neighbor's porch; admiring a string of ducks shot by an uncle for a yummy dinner; being startled to see my little brother halfway up the windmill tower; Mother soaking my nail-punctured foot in her magic potion; the fresh smell of corn ears, just picked; winning a box of chocolates and a valentine word game in third grade... These and many other memories make me proud of my rural heritage.

Dorothy Klahn
Denver, Colorado

The Barn Was My Escape from Reality

Looking back on my life as a boy around the year 1944, the very first thing that comes to mind is the old barn. I used it for more things than it was designed for. Our old barn was built from rough, unpainted lumber with cracks in it that had spread as they dried. As I remember the lower floor had six stalls. We used two stalls to keep the plow mules in, one for a cow, and another for visitors' animals or a calf if we happened to have one. One of the two stalls on the east end was used for equipment work and storage, and the second one was used to store peanuts or sometimes to dry potatoes. The loft or upper part was my domain.

As a young boy, it seemed the loft was a whole different world. We had one section with baled hay. One section had raked hay. One section would have cottonseed or corn if our crib was overfilled.

In the section that had the baled hay, I made secret passages that I thought no enemy could possibly locate. I could go all the way through the maze to portholes through the cracks on the north side. There, with my make-believe weapons, I could protect the fort. In the part with the loose hay I could dive from the upper rafters or I would jump from my bomber, aflame over enemy territory. I would have corncobs hidden in many different places for the battle that would take place on Sunday after church and lunch.

The most important part of my old castle was the role it played as an escape from pressures. Even now when I see a barn on a rainy or dreary day, it really carries me back. I can remember sitting on the hay in the cool rain, looking out over a peaceful day. I would watch the rain and many thoughts would cross my mind, including how many of my cousins and uncles would return from the war alive. I would wonder if the war would last long enough for me to be a part of it or if the enemy won what they would do to us here. Those question have all been answered now, but many still remain unanswered. I wonder if we could think through most of them if the old barn still stood.

Clyde J. Posey
Cleveland, Alabama

We Took Everything for Granted

I grew up on an Iowa farm along with two brothers and three sisters during the late teens, '20s and '30s. Our 420-acre farm, which was under the control of my father and mother, was a completely diversified operation.

Our dad's main interest was livestock and the planting and harvesting of crops. Mom's was household chores, gardening, canning and care of a growing family of six children, of which I was the third. The precious memories of those first 18 years are without a doubt the ones that I hold most dear, and the best of my 78 years on this earth.

We kids had fun growing up, but we also had our share of chores and work to perform. There was always time for play and we were given free reign to use our imaginations in any constructive way to build "toys" or whatever for us and the neighbor kids to use.

One thing in particular that provided amusement and fun for the Hager Kids as well as our peers in the neighborhood was an old, stripped-down buggy that had seen better days. We removed the shaves, the box and seats, leaving nothing but the wheels and frame to hold it together. A long, light link chain was fastened to the axle near each front wheel to steer this contraption as you would guide a horse. We would push it out to a pasture that had a steep hill, where we would coast down at what we considered dangerous speeds. There were moving hazards to avoid, such as pigs and calves, which made the ride even more thrilling.

All the neighbor kids, including us, enjoyed winter sports, such as ice skating and sledding down that same hill. We also enjoyed horseback riding.

Were we happy? You bet we were. We took everything for granted and were satisfied with what we had. As the old saying goes, "Who could ask for anything more."

Francis E. Hager

Sun City, Arizona

Runt and the She-Devil

I daresay that the memories of those of us who were actually raised on a family farm—especially those who labored on rice farms in the deep South—will not sound as romantic as those who were only occasional visitors of one. I was the eldest of three brothers and when we weren't in school or church, we were more than likely engaged in some sort of farm activity. Such was the case for most all of the farm boys in our neck of the woods. We worked hard from "can see to can't see" as they say, raising rice, soybeans and cattle.

All of this is not to say there aren't an abundance of fond and pleasant memories mingled with those of sweat and toil. A cool dip in our pond at the end of a dusty summer's day of work, feeling the wind in my face as I galloped across a green pasture on my favorite horse, gazing upon the "north 40" and watching a sea of golden rice waving at the setting sun, knowing that I'd had a hand in bringing that field to life, those are the farm memories that dwell in my heart.

A good laugh can be a real godsend in those times on a farm when the days of hard work seem to roll by like an endless train. I remember one such occasion quite vividly.

It occurred during mid-August of my 16th year. My brothers, Junior and Runt, who were 14 and 11 respectfully, and I were herding cattle from one pasture to another, each of us mounted on our favorite horse. As is often the case, Junior and I were easily annoyed by the presence of our younger sibling. That morning, being seared by the blazing sun overhead while horse flies buzzed all around, Runt's ability to aggravate Junior and I was doubly effective. Throughout the morning he had constantly jabbered about his horse being prettier and faster than ours—statements that were true but nonetheless annoying—amidst complaints of being thirsty, hungry or hot and sometimes all three at once. Needless to say, Junior and I were near the breaking point.

Just about the time I was ready to ask the good Lord, "Why me?" I spotted an old mossy-horned cow on the edge of a narrow thicket of pines and brush that skirted the field. I was reining my horse in old mossy-horn's direction, when all of a sudden Runt went flying at her on his galloping mount, shouting confidently, "I'll git 'er."

Junior, staying close to our bunched herd, asked casually, "Ain't that the one Daddy calls the 'She-Devil'?" I nodded my head as a smile began spreading on my lips.

Taking heed of Runt's charging advance, old She-Devil slipped into the thicket, disappearing from our view. "This I gotta' see," Junior remarked with a shake of his head, as Runt and his trusty steed became enveloped by the dense undergrowth. For about 10 or 15 seconds we heard a lot of shouting, mooing and wood being trampled under hoof. Suddenly, Runt emerged from the far side of the thicket, his lathered horse running to beat the band and a hint of childish shock highlighting his freckled face. Two beats behind them came the hard-charging She-Devil, bellowing angrily at her would-be assailants as they rapidly left her behind. She quickly gave up the chase and commenced to wander over in the direction of our herd, her appetite for excitement apparently satisfied.

Junior and I exchanged an amused glance that rapidly evolved into full-blown laughter. For a good two minutes we chuckled and slapped our knees as our eyes followed the shrinking forms of Runt and his horse.

Finally, I managed to stop laughing long enough to remark, "Yep. He sure enough had the fastest horse." Then our laughter rang out again, and so it rings to this day.

Randy Ritter
New Iberia, Louisiana

Saturday Nights of Long Ago

We provided our own entertainment when I was growing up just after the Depression on our family farm.

"Saturday Night Live" was a hot summer evening sitting on the porch with Dad and Mom. In the early twilight, we fanned the hot, stifling muggy air, hoping for a tiny breeze to relieve the heat.

The pale moon rode high in the sky among stars that stood out like sparkly diamonds against black velvet, while frogs croaked to each other on the banks of the creek below the garden in the meadow and fireflies twinkled in the heavy air.

A low, gentle moo was heard from a cow nearby making sure her calf was safe and comfortable for the night. A disgruntled hen clucked her disgust as a roost mate took some of her space and disturbed her sleep.

The nearest light was more than a mile away. I felt like the blackness would swallow me as I sat there with the warm air caressing my face. The nighttime seemed friendly as Dad identified its sounds: the bullfrog, cicadas or katydids, tree frogs and others.

As I wiggled to find a more comfortable position, I squashed an inquisitive June bug. That helped to make up for the one that had somehow gotten into my bed and crawled up my arm just as I had gotten to sleep after what seemed like hours of tossing and turning on those hot, white sheets the previous night.

I pumped water out of the old hand pump into the washpan. The water came from the far depths and was icy cold. Goosebumps ran all over me as I plunged the stubbed toes and nettle-ridden feet of my barefoot days into that delicious coolness.

If there was money left after necessities were bought with the egg and milk checks, Dad would purchase a case of Double Cola and a 50-pound block of ice. We would sit in the darkness and sip the cooled nectar with the chipped ice.

Mother always had a saying for everything, and when she wanted to tell me something, but I wasn't supposed to tell the world, she would say, "Just between you and me and the gatepost." There's something about sitting together in the dark as a family and sharing your deepest thoughts without any interruptions that brings a closeness you never forget. And that's "Just between you and me and the gatepost."

Neoma Foreman
Walker, Missouri

A Summer Full of Memories

I was 10 years old when our family moved to the country. We had a three-room (shotgun) house. We had no electricity, water or plumbing. We did have a wood heater, kerosene lamps, a cook-stove, and a path to the outhouse. Both my parents had to work in town that summer, and I was left in charge of three younger siblings. We had a neighbor a quarter-mile away, so I knew there was help nearby if I needed someone.

That summer was the best memory of my childhood. There were so many new experiences to be tasted. A shallow spring-fed creek flowed nearby, which afforded wading or sitting in the cool water looking for special rocks, as well as the fun of trying to catch minnows. We were watchful of crawdads. We had been warned they could pinch, so no pinches. However, we discovered a few ant hills that could make us dance.

In a grove of persimmon trees, among the young saplings, we played cowboys and Indians. We climbed on those trees and rode them like horses. Up and down we went; even my 4-year-old sister would squeal with joy.

My mother helped me plant my first flower bed that summer. I had the most beautiful "Old Maid" zinnias. In my memory they are the prettiest flowers I've ever grown. Mother also began to teach me to cook. Corn bread and pinto beans were my offering to the table on Saturdays. On Sundays after church our aunts, uncles and cousins came for dinner. We sat under shade trees, watched ball games or games of horseshoes or played hide-and-seek. Those were fun times.

One day late that summer when I was looking forward to the beginning of school again, my brother came running to the back door. He was shouting, "I found a cat, I found a cat!" We girls all followed him out to the little barn that stood on a few large supporting stones, leaving lots of open space underneath. We all got down on our hands and knees and sure enough, we could see movement there in the shadows. My brother said, "Let's throw rocks at it and chase it away." A new adventure! We all picked up a rock. Several rocks hit the side of the barn and a few actually went underneath, none of which hit the target. However, we did alarm our adversary, which turned out to be a skunk, and he let us know that the war was over. We quickly retreated, and I guess the skunk went the other way. Fortunately, none of his scent landed on us.

Thinking back on that first summer in the country, it always brings such a rush of feelings—love, companionship, the cool wind on our faces as we rode our tree horses, the sheer joy of splashing in the water, the feeling of pride when Daddy said "that corn bread is almost as good as your mama's," and oh, I wish I could find some "Old Maid" zinnia seeds.

For me, the summer I was 10 held new smells, sights, sounds and the experience of having my work turn into pretty flowers or a pan of corn bread. Perhaps the joy I felt then set my heart to singing and gave me a good start on my life as a country girl.

Anna Brumback
Stilwell, Oklahoma

Bath Time Mischief

In 1940 there were still many farms in Illinois without electricity or bath facilities. I grew up with nine other children on one of those farms.

We bathed on Saturday nights in a washtub behind the wood-burning kitchen range. The kitchen would be closed off, with the younger children bathing first and my high school age sister bathing last.

One Saturday night after the younger children had bathed and my big sister was still relaxing in the washtub, two of us younger sisters slipped out the front door, ran around to the back of the house and knocked loudly on the back door. In those days, the back door was used when friends and neighbors came calling.

Needless to say, my big sister lost no time in getting out of the washtub and running for safety. With no place to go, she tried to hide in the supply closet where the milk strainer hung on the door.

Since there was actually no room for a person to hide in the closet, the milk strainer was knocked from its resting place with much clatter and landed on her bare foot.

When big sister learned the knocking was only a trick played on her by two of her mischievous younger sisters, she was very upset and threatened to remove our names from her Christmas gift list.

Margie Van Meter
Lewistown, Missouri

———■———

Chapter 3: Creatures Great and Small

Berries for Bossy

Almost blackberry time again. Anyone who has lived in the state of Washington knows that they grow wild there. How my mouth was watering for some nice fresh berries. I had some canned and some blackberry jam but they weren't the same as fresh ones.

I had noticed some berries turning colors and I thought I could get enough ripe ones for dinner; of course that meant eating a few myself as I picked.

Grabbing a pail I went down in the pasture along the creek. I found green ones but no black ones. I guessed it was too early yet.

I turned to go back when I noticed a patch where the berries had been picked. I followed the trail. Occasionally I would see a ripe berry, which I ate myself. Now I wondered, who would come into our pasture and pick the berries when there was lots of them along the road. After they turned ripe there would be enough for everyone, but I wanted the first ones myself. I decided to follow the trail and see if I could spot who was doing this. It was infuriating to me.

As I turned around the bend of the creek, to my surprise I saw the culprits. It was our cow, Bossy, and her calf, Blackie. They were going along eating only the ripe berries.

Evelyn Williams-Hall
Sioux City, Iowa

43

Ducklings, Peas and Pillows

We began a whole new lifestyle when we moved our 19-foot trailer from beneath the big oaks in Coon Hill schoolyard to the undeveloped area on Kinch Road we bought to permanently build on in 1944. Long before the well driller drove our 149-foot well I ordered 15 ducklings to be shipped by parcel post. I just couldn't wait. Bob, my husband, told me they needed very little protection from the wind and weather. He got me an old but very big tractor tire to construct a temporary home for them in.

The rural mail carrier arrived with the ducklings on a bright sunny morning about three weeks later. It was such fun to pick them out of the tight little box and feel the warm, soft, featherlike fur on their bodies. Their beaks were so bright and intriguing! They could snap at and catch a fly. I put stones in a flat dish with enough water to drink and submerge their tiny heads in but not enough to drown in. Just as I finished Bob called and asked me if I could run into town and exchange a set of undersized rings for the engine he was overhauling. I gave one last look at the tiny yellow ducklings and reluctantly drove into town, picked up the parts and returned home. He thanked me and I immediately rushed to my ducklings.

As I approached their makeshift shelter I could hear no sounds. I ran faster. Inside, the place was empty. The feed and water were just as I left them, but the ducklings were gone! I hastened back to where my husband was working and inquired, "Where did you put my ducklings? I left them in my square galvanized laundry tub. It is empty. There is not one in sight." He shook his head and replied, "I have been working right here all the time. I didn't touch them."

Together we returned to the empty tub. I still couldn't believe it! We walked around searching for some clue. In a distant dark corner, a good 20 feet away, we spied one lone, limp duckling almost concealed in the opening of a small underground burrow. Bob bent down, carefully picked it up, and looked it over. There, under its wing, was a tiny spot of blood. "A weasel! Well, I'll be!"

he exclaimed. "She must have killed every one of them and carried them off to her babies. You must have surprised her causing her to drop this one. I'll fix her!" He backed our pickup close to the burrow, attached an old vacuum hose to the exhaust pipe, and pushed the opposite end into the opening. He turned on the engine and let the motor run for a good two hours. He assured me that we would have no more trouble from that family!

Two weeks later we were expecting new ducklings. It just happened that a neighbor stopped in and saw us getting ready. She hesitated and remarked, "It is not my business to tell you what to do, but what you really need is my Mother Pekins Duck. She had a nest full of eggs. Only two hatched because the rest were destroyed by a stray dog. There is a 50-50 chance that if we sneak your ducklings under her during the night she will think they belong to her. She just might accept them, and a sassy mother duck is almost as good as a dog! You are welcome to bring her over here. She would either accept them or reject them. Come after dark tonight and we will move her."

Bob quickly constructed a better shelter from some pieces of scrap lumber. We got into our pickup after nightfall and drove down to the neighbor's farm. Cynthia hoisted the mother duck, sitting on her own two ducklings, crate and all just as they had hatched, into our pickup. We drove carefully and quietly home. We set the crate down and put our ducklings under her one by one. I stroked her across the back. She seemed to like it. She raised herself on her feet, balancing and resting her body on her legs. As we added ducklings she spread her wings, making more space underneath her. At last number 15 was under her! My knees felt weak. I got up and made my way back to our trailer. I kept wondering, "What would happen in the morning? Would she accept them? She might attack them and even kill them." It was a long night.

In the morning I rushed out to look. It was long before 6 o'clock but she was ahead of me. There she was standing, then moving carefully, and quacking softly. I stopped some distance back. Something told me she was the mother now. She was in full charge. I knew that I wasn't needed or wanted for a duckling sitter. It was my job to keep feed and water handy. They ate continually like little pigs, scooping their wet mash into their mouths like miniature steam shovels. They outgrew the tire and we concocted a second shelter.

One day I found two lying on their sides struggling to rise. I stood them up but they fell down again and again as fast as I could stand them up. My husband said, "The water must be deep enough for them to poke their heads into it to wash the insects out of their ears and eyes. They are old enough to swim on the pond now." I opened the 18-inch high chicken-wire fence to let them out. They didn't know they were free. I didn't think I should butt in and drive them out. Bob said, "Leave them alone. They will find out sooner or later!" I was dying to see them get into the pond but after standing there a long time I decided I had to get to work. Later in the forenoon I had to run into town for some engine parts. I checked the duck family. Everybody was fine!

When I returned home I went to check on them immediately. I expected to see Mother Pekins and her brood of 17, but there was not one duck or duckling in sight. I stopped dead still. Where were they? I shifted my gaze, scanning the whole backyard. There, to the right of and halfway back to the pond, Mother Pekins, in all her beautiful white ruffled feathers, stood. No! She was waddling around and around! Her head was tilted down; her eyes were staring at the center of the circle. I hastened toward her. All the while her quacks were sending distressful tones. If a duck can sound desperate she did. As I advanced toward the spot where she kept her eyes focused, I saw an old fence-post hole. Looking down into the hole I saw a pile of ducklings. The tall grass had hidden the hole. She must have stepped around it, but the ducklings had followed a more direct route and fallen in. I bent down and lifted them out one by one. They were all alive and none the worse for the experience. She called out a message in a new tone. She turned toward the pond and waddled right down to it with every duckling following in a beautiful long line. She stepped into the water. Without one hesitation every duckling followed! They were floating, swimming and bobbing their heads up and down in the water. One climbed on the mother's back. They kept climbing on and sliding off, and they really had to squeeze when the sixth one wedged itself upon her back!

The days and nights fairly flew. It seemed to me that I could almost see them growing longer, taller and bigger. Their feathers were all white now. They were about three-fourths of their adult size. It was getting harder to keep them inside their pen. They had pretty much devoured most of the vegetation. There was no doubt about it; we were simply going to have to build a better fence.

We continued to work on our house, and the ducklings continued to grow. One day when I went to check on them, they were nowhere in sight. Instinct told me to look in the garden. I ran. Pushing apart the green foliage of the grape leaves that hid my garden from view, I saw what no gardener wishes to see! Those ducks were working their way down my five rows of peas. Behind the culprits was bare ground; in front of then stood my 20-inch, knee-high, ready to harvest crop. Every second more and more of my peas were disappearing. I ran around them, getting in front of the oncoming herd. I yelled and hollered; I flailed my arms and waved my hat. I frightened then back into their pen, located the hole, did another repair job and left feeling very downhearted about the loss of my peas.

Ten weeks had passed. The ducks were ready to pluck. My grandmother had often told me about her life in Bohemia before she came to America. Her job as a young girl had been to herd and care for the ducks and geese. At the age of 10 weeks they plucked the down from them alive. The fowls grew a second crop of feathers before winter. This was a real financial boost to the family as many feathers were required for pillows and feather beds. Any not needed by the family were sold. I needed pillows badly; I decided on following her plan!

I held the miserable, wet, smelly ducks between my knees and legs while I plucked. It was very slow, tedious work but I kept at it. I thought of my grandmother and their pond with the big, black cherry tree on the north end of it back in Bohemia. I didn't exactly like the smell but I kept thinking about the fun I'd had raising them. I was glad when they were plucked. They looked mighty funny and naked.

Summer weather gave way to autumn. The ducklings were full grown now. Their bodies were again covered with down and new feathers. The weather was cold; they put on weight rapidly. The family came on Thanksgiving Day and the roast duck was tasty. As for the feathers, nobody ever dreamt that in 1994 I would be using those two big, soft, fluffy down pillows I made from those ducks in 1944. I hope that someday one of my grandchildren will want and cherish these pillows!

Lucille Stanek Jenkins

Jackson, Michigan

We Barely Escaped the Bull

I was raised on the plains of South Dakota. My sister Hazel and I had to go a couple of miles to the school bus line. Our transportation was our bicycle; me on the mid-bar and Hazel riding and peddling it. She was a high school freshman and I was in the seventh grade.

Our neighbor had cattle in his field across from our home. He usually had Herefords, but that year he had raised a yearling Holstein bull.

As we left the house one morning we noticed the bull by the neighbor's fence, bellowing at our cows. We were always very afraid of bulls and we hoped he would not follow along inside his fence. He remained there bellowing for a while. We had covered about half the distance to an unused rural schoolhouse three-fourths of a mile from our home. Suddenly the bull seemed to move like lightning as he saw us pass on the road. He rushed along inside his fence, bellowing furiously. Hazel pedaled as fast as possible and told me to keep an eye on the bull. That fence was a regular woven wire with three strands of barbed wire at the top. We had no idea whether the bull could get through or over it.

We were nearing the unused schoolhouse when I saw the bull back off, rush at the fence and sail right over it. He galloped toward us and I jumped off the bike, making it easier for Hazel to wheel it onto the school grounds and up to the building. We were afraid the schoolhouse was locked, and it was, but the entry door was not. In a panic we dragged the bike up the steps and into the entry and slammed the door right in the bull's face! He roared and pawed on the steps and small porch. We were breathless and scared almost to death. The bull pushed and pawed on the door; it had no lock and we tried to hold it shut. We prayed out loud for God to help us. We feared the door would not hold much longer and we were helplessly trapped.

We had endured this for about 15 minutes when we heard a car horn and noticed a lessening of the bull's activity. We had a neighbor who lived in the opposite direction from the schoolhouse, and we heard her voice calling to us. She yelled for us to leave the bike and to try to come out and get in her car. We opened the door a crack and saw her car pulled right up at the steps. She got out of her car and the bull started for her, but she had a pitchfork and he paused a bit over that. In that moment, on the other side of the car, we grabbed the door open and jumped in. The neighbor got in the driver's side and we roared off with the bull chasing the car for a while before he gave up. The neighbor took us to the school bus line, but we were so upset we might as well have missed that day of school.

The bull's owner was informed about this incident and he had the animal shipped off to the packing house the next day.

God certainly did answer our prayer for help. Twenty-seven years later as I talked with the neighbor about rescuing us she said, "It must have been the Lord, I couldn't see the road or the schoolhouse from inside my home, but that morning I happened to go out early to feed my chickens and I saw you go into the entry with the bull after you."

Eunice Hoien Dahlgren
Sweet Home, Oregon

The Fascinating Fundraisers

When I was in high school, I needed to earn money for college. My parents and I came up with the idea of raising geese. We didn't know too much about it, but we read all we could and talked to people who raised them. We bought a few White Embden and a few Toulouse goslings from the Murray McMurray Hatchery in Webster City, Iowa. Every year we had more geese. We started hatching our own. One year we had more than 100, all of them named.

We found the geese to be quite interesting creatures. They liked to nibble at everything, including valve stems and house wires. We had to wear jean jackets with metal buttons that were pressed into the material because the geese would gnaw at regular buttons and snip them right off. When a goose couldn't saw off the metal ones, he would look quizzically up at me as if to say, "How come I can't snip this off?"

The geese hated to see us leave. They would run along beside the car as we were driving away, bite at the tires, and scold us. When we came back home, they would raise their heads in the air and trumpet with joy.

Another interesting thing was how the geese all bunched together tightly in time of danger. One of them would spot a hawk in the sky, sound the alarm, and all would come running. They must have thought there was safety in numbers. If they were different ages, they would start fighting as soon as the danger was over.

A comical thing happened one day. We looked out the window and saw one of the geese crawling on his belly as tight to the ground as he could get. His neck was stretched straight out, and one eye was focused on the sky. We wondered what in the world he saw. We listened and looked up to see an airplane flying very low. That goose was sure that plane was headed right for him.

The geese made good lawn mowers. We just fenced off the area we wanted mowed. In a short time the grass would be all nibbled off. Then we would move the fence to a different area. Once we didn't have time to move the fence right away. We pulled grass for them and threw it in the pen. They would all make a mad dash for it. In no time it would all be gone. My mother got a mischievous streak one day and decided to throw in some onion tops. The geese dashed for them and just as quickly spewed them out, shaking their heads back and forth in disgust. It was so funny.

Joy J. Palmer
Forest City, Iowa

The Mysterious Disappearing Milk

Unexpected things do happen on farms. It was wintertime and very cold. There was a lot of snow with a frozen crust. All animals and poultry were given protection as much as possible. The cattle were bedded in the long cattle shed, which was open on the south side. Any sort of windbreak was a big help against a howling north wind in Kansas. The six pig shoats that ran in the feedlot with the cattle found a place in the end of the shed. When fodder corn was fed, cattle often knock off ears and some cattlemen let a few pigs run with the cattle to get those ears. Tanks froze so that ice had to be cut to let the livestock drink. This was long before the time of oil or electric heaters on tanks to keep a constant supply of drinking water.

Milking by hand was a morning and evening chore. One morning Old Bess, as we called the big roan cow, had no milk. That was strange because she always gave most of a pail. At evening time she gave the usual amount or a little more. And so it went for a week or more, with no milk in the morning. What was the reason? Surely it couldn't be the cold winter weather. One night Dad was up a couple of times to check something at the barn. As he passed the cattle shed, he heard a sucking noise. He turned his lantern toward the noise. What do you suppose he saw? There sat a red-and-white spotted shoat pig sucking Bess. He sat like a dog and was surely enjoying a warm meal.

As you can guess, Dad put that rascal of a pig in a pen away from the cattle, and Bess gave her usual bucket of milk each morning.

Mary Worley
Azalea, Oregon

Our Chester White Hogs

Our 100-acre farm was surrounded by other farms, because my grandparents homesteaded it when they were married. My father ended up being a farmer with a family of six. He married a teacher who became a diligent farm wife.

When I was 2 years old, a baby brother arrived, but he only lived a few days, so I grew up lonely.

My heartstrings were woven around this little farm. I attended a rural school that closed at the end of two years; after that I went to a new consolidated school.

The Oak Ridge Stock Farm, as it was named, provided well for us. My dad raised only Chester White hogs, mostly for breeding purposes. They were real pets because we handled them well and they were a source of good income.

At a fair one time, my dad bought a Chester White boar to add to his herd. Advanced Giant, as he was called, was a real pet. He measured six feet in length from the tip of his nose to the end of his tail. He was a real show hog and a friendly one. Every kid who came to visit had a ride on his back. Lots of people felt that Dad had paid too much for him, since the price was $75, but after having him for a long while he was sold on the market, and he got his money back.

Madonna L. Storla
Postville, Iowa

Orphan Calf

This was the $64 question: Out of 64 cows, which one did the orphan calf belong to? If animals could only talk they could have solved the problem.

Last Monday I changed my clothes, locked the kitchen door and started walking toward the barnyard. I was walking slowly because I was meditating on the wise words of an old saying, "Never run. Walk, because as you walk along you'll solve many of your problems before you get there."

When I arrived at the pole barn I leaned against a wooden gate and gazed absentmindedly across the empty barnyard. Something was different; something was wrong. There, in the far corner inside the barnyard, lay a small black object. I climbed over the gate wondering, "What is going on here?" As I walked closer and closer I knew. Sure enough! Curled up into a snug little ball, sleeping in the fresh warm sunshine, lay a newborn black Angus calf.

I went on about my business of fixing the fence. I thought, "Its mother will come and pick it up later." It is quite common for a mother cow to hide her calf for two or three days before she takes it into a big herd.

After a couple of hours passed the calf got up and meandered wobbly to the fence. It stood there looking at me. After finishing my job I left. It was still standing there.

When I returned on the second morning it was still there. I worked around inside the barn. After a while she worked her way up closer to me. I began to wonder, "Where is the mother?" As the day wore on no mother appeared. By late afternoon I was getting concerned.

Later, around 4:00 o'clock, I got on my tractor and drove out to the cornfield, where I hooked the chopper on and attached the empty wagon to it. I drove around and around the field until the wagon was full. I unhooked the chopper and left it in the cornfield. I took the full wagon and hauled it to the pasture for the day's feeding. The herd saw me coming and rushed toward me. I climbed off the tractor, hurriedly unpinned the wagon, very quickly hopped back on the tractor and drove away to avoid being trampled by them. As they circled around the wagon to eat the chopped sudan grass I drove around and around behind them observing them. I did not spot one cow that looked like the eligible mother to the orphan in my barnyard.

"There's no mother here? What is going on?" I pondered. Then I spoke aloud, "It's definitely time for me to do something. That calf is hungry. Time is running out!"

I put a heavy foot on the gas pedal. The tractor took off like a scared rabbit, jarring and bumping me over every stone and the gully all the way home. I hopped off the tractor and into my car.

Remembering the feed store would close at 9:00 o'clock, I knew I had to get there quickly; 20 miles in 20 minutes would be a close call. All I could think of was that the little orphan was dehydrating and getting weaker every minute. She would never make it till morning; I was probably too late now. She could not hold out much longer. They were just ready to lock the door as I pulled up. I ran!

Once inside I rushed straight to the agriculture department where the calf supplies were. I bought a nursing nipple to put on a pop bottle and $30 worth of calf feed. I didn't bother to purchase any other items.

The minute I got home I read the directions, prepared the formula and put the nipple on the bottle. I didn't waste any time getting to the barnyard. She was lying on the ground with her head and legs curled under her. I thought she was dead. I picked her up and helped her stand, but she kept going limp and slipping back down. Finally, I braced her against a couple of hay bales and held her with my legs. Using my thumb and third finger of my right hand to hold her mouth open I tried to tickle her tongue with my index finger. At first she paid no attention to the nipple but finally, just as I was about to give up, she began to suckle and pull on the nipple. After a little more coaxing I removed my index finger and she emptied the bottle. She'd had her first pint! I rubbed her ear and patted her head. As I released my hold she slipped down on the straw by the hay bales and curled up. I patted her little head and fondled her ears and said, "I'll see you in the morning." I left feeling greatly relieved.

When she was a week old I put her milk into a pail without the nipple. She played 'possum for a few minutes; I poked her head lower into the milk. She gave a little snort and shook her head, giving me a milk shower. Soon she drank greedily and emptied the bucket. It was many days before her tummy was no longer hollow, her eyes sparkled and her hair took on a soft new luster. She soon came running when she saw me approaching. She looked pretty cute the day she jumped over a bale to get to me. I honestly felt a little flattered when she began following me around like a dog.

Neither she nor I were looking for her mother anymore. We gave up; she was on her own.

I'll probably never know the answer to the $64 question. If only animals could talk... she just might be able to tell me which one of those cows was her mother. Frankly neither of us give a darn!

Lucille Stanek Jenkins
Jackson, Michigan

Chicken Stories

I grew up on a farm with my parents and nine brothers and sisters. I was sixth in line. As we grew up to handle responsibilities each one had to do his or her part.

My area of responsibility was in the chicken yard. We raised chickens from start to finish. They were a large part of our livelihood. Nature created the hen to become broody in the summertime; she quit laying and sat on her nest like a dummy for weeks at a time if allowed. We put broody hens on a nest of 15 carefully selected large eggs. We had nest apartments of about 12 in a row. Each hen had her own apartment where she settled in for her three weeks of brooding. She sat patiently, as if in a trance. Once each day I put her in a coop where she had her feed, water, dust bath and elimination; she never soiled her nest.

After three weeks of this, we listened closely and we could hear a little tapping going on inside the egg. Soon a little hole appeared. As the chick kept pecking, the opening grew larger. Finally the shell broke in two and out came a little wet chick. It soon dried and became a beautiful, bright-eyed fluffy little ball.

The hen and her chicks were housed in a larger coop. Soon they roamed the yard, garden and orchard searching for grasshoppers, beetles and anything that suited their fancy in addition to their usual diet of small grains and water.

As they grew larger, the day came when the cockerels were large enough for the frying pan. To catch them we used a stick with an extended wire with a hook bent on the end to snare them by the leg. They then went to the chopping block; this part I did not like. Next they were immersed in very hot water, which made it easy to remove their feathers.

After being washed and cut into serving pieces, the chicken was ready for the frying pan, which had plenty of pork fat in it. Along with new potatoes, peas and pie made with fresh-picked cherries, this was a dinner to be remembered.

The pullets were saved and kept for laying hens. As the laying hens grew old they quit laying. Then was the time to cull out the non-layers, which was not hard to do. They were taken to the market and sold. These sales provided us with money for new clothes, dresses, shoes or coats, which we often purchased from the Sears and Roebuck or Montgomery Ward catalogs.

Our chicken yard included turkeys. One old gobbler didn't like me; often he would sneak up behind me and attack. One day I picked up a stick and threw it at him. To my surprise my aim was so good he hit the ground. I hadn't meant to kill him and was sorry. However, he recovered and learned a lesson. It was a long time before he bothered me again.

One day Mother and I were sitting on the porch when an old rooster strutted in front of us. Mother looked him over and said we should have him for dinner. This old rooster was ugly; he had lost his tail feathers and parts of his body were bare and wrinkled and his legs had long spurs. I declared I was not going to eat any of that meat. In a family of 10 children Mother couldn't pay attention to such notions.

After the rooster meat was browned and put into the waterless cooker with onions and other appropriate spices, the kitchen filled with a delicious aroma. As the cooker valves clicked the smell grew more and more delicious. This hungry girl was sorry for the vow she had made and would gladly have eaten that meat, but she was true to her word and ate only the gravy. Mother, bless her heart, didn't even remind me of my rashness.

Mrs. Arthur E. Koehn
Macon, Mississippi

Prodigal Pig

In December of 1990, my husband and his brother were repairing hog gates. In the process of opening and closing gates, one pen of sows got loose. The men were able to get all of the sows back in except one. She just refused to be driven. The men chased her all over. By that time I was out there to help too. The sow got buried in one huge snowdrift after another. She finally started heading in the right direction. Our relief was short-lived, because she took off running for my brother-in-law's place across the road. We chased her around there for a while. My sister-in-law came out to help too. Finally the sow got caught in some hay rakes. By that time she was exhausted. When we tried to get her out, she lunged viciously at us. We had no choice but to leave her there. We hoped she would come back on her own if she got rested up and grew hungry.

The next day there was evidence that she had been around the corncrib. However, the following day there was no sign of her. The next afternoon the neighbor stopped by and asked if we were missing a sow. We said, "Yes, as a matter of fact."

My husband and I went over to survey the situation. We decided to attempt a night rescue. There were no fences at that place. We thought maybe we could back the trailer up to the machine shed and use some gates to corral her. We knew it would be tricky. The sow had made a nest under some grain-handling equipment nearby.

That night before we went over we prayed, "Lord, help us to get that sow in the trailer. Help her to want to go in." We parked the trailer in the driveway so we could check out whether the sow was still there. When she saw the flashlights, she came tearing out like a madman. Then she spied the trailer. She came running toward it and then went past it onto the road. We prayed, "Lord, help her to come back." Just then, she turned around and came back to the trailer and started sniffing and grunting. My brother-in-law opened the door carefully and coaxed her, and she jumped right in. She was ready to go home. We didn't even have to use the gates.

Joy J. Palmer

Forest City, Iowa

Our Cow, Lady

We were going to get our first cow! Were we ever excited. Jake, my husband, had made a deal with Joe, the fellow he worked for, for a cow. So much of his wages each week would go toward the cow, which he would bring home once she was paid for.

We already had a dozen chickens and now the cow. Maybe we could get our own farm yet.

The day finally came when our cow was coming home. We were all waiting when Joe drove up and they unloaded the cow and put her in the barn.

The next question the kids had was, "What are we going to name her?" To me Bossy seemed too common, so we finally decided on Lady.

We had a lovely big yard full of green grass, and I thought that she should be outside. But Jake said, "I'll be home tomorrow and then we'll put her out and I can watch her better."

I felt bad, but not knowing much about cows I thought I'd better do what Jake said, though I thought I had enough sense to take care of a cow.

It was close to the Fourth of July. We could hear firecrackers popping and there was a picnic coming up. I figured I had better start planning what to fix. First I decided to go get the mail.

As I sat under the trees reading the mail, I thought, "It's such a beautiful day I am going to let Lady out. It's so nice I'll let her eat grass while I read the mail."

I found a rope and tied it around her neck and led her out of the barn. She rolled her eyes and gave a soft moo, as if to say "Thank you."

The children soon tired of watching Lady eat and found other things to do.

Somehow Joey found a firecracker and managed to light it. Lady gave a start, kicked up her heels and took off down the road.

I ran as hard as I could after her but she had disappeared. Boy, was I in for it. What was I going to do? My nearest neighbor was a half-mile down the road. Maybe Lady was there with his cows.

I cautioned the children to stay out of the road and to watch while I went to see. I had to get Lady home before Jake got home. He would be furious.

I started down the road when a car stopped. I wanted to run when a voice said, "Lady, do you know where... ?" I looked at the car real close because that voice sounded like Pop. It couldn't be. He was in Iowa. It was Pop and Mom! They were driving out to see their son in Oregon and decided to look me up.

I explained what had happened and Pop said, "Don't worry now. We'll go see if we can find the cow."

Mom took over the children and started lunch. We found Lady with the neighbor's cows. Pop helped me lead her up the road and we put Lady in the barn.

We went in to eat but Bobby, my 3-year-old, was missing. We called and called. Finally we found him asleep in the pasture. He had tried to follow me down the road by going through the pasture. He had gotten tired, sat down and dropped off to sleep.

Finally, everyone accounted for, we had our lunch and a nice visit, despite a bad beginning. I wondered if I would ever be a good farmer's wife.

Evelyn Williams-Hall
Sioux City, Iowa

The Angry Cow

Our dairy herd was docile most of the time with the exception of one cow that became dangerous when she had a new calf.

One evening I was coming from school and I heard a snort. Here she came—I ran as fast as I could to get inside the corncrib. I barely got the door closed when she hit it with a bang.

It was two hours later when my folks came home and Dad had to use a pitchfork to get her away from the corncrib door. Three days later she was as quiet as could be.

Madonna L. Storla
Postville, Iowa

Honkers Go Bonkers

This is a rather "shocking" story. We kept geese in the old hog house. We gave them water in a round metal pan that we placed on the ground near the windmill. One day we noticed that the geese didn't seem to want to drink out of that pan. They would stick their necks out to get a drink, and then all of a sudden jump back.

About the same time we were having trouble in the house. When Mom and I used the sink in the basement bathroom we got a shock. We kept telling Dad about it, and he just laughed. One day Dad used that sink when he had bare feet. He came flying upstairs saying, "You know what? I got a shock from that sink in the basement." We said, "That's what we've been telling you." Dad decided right then and there to call an electrician.

The electrician found a short in some wiring on the windmill. The windmill was probably 600-800 feet from the house. After the electrical problem was fixed, we had no more trouble. We couldn't figure that out. How could a problem at the windmill affect the house when it was so far away? The windmill wiring had nothing to do with the house wiring, and the water was not piped to the house either. I still don't know the answer, except that when I dowsed for water, I found that the vein of water from that well went right under that corner of the house.

After considerable hesitation the geese went back to drinking out of the metal pan.

Joy J. Palmer
Forest City, Iowa

Outsmarting a Bull

It was one lovely summer day in June. Our first cutting hay was stacked in huge mows in our barn ready for the animals to munch on the next winter. I was 10 years old and the youngest of a family of 15. The oldest ones were married and not living at home.

We had a boat ride planned for that night on a neighbor's pond, and I was helping my brothers and sisters haul manure out of the box stalls in the barn. We were all in a hurry to finish our job and get the chores done so we could start early with our boat ride. As my brother went to unload the last load of manure, I went with him to bring the cows home for evening milking. Like any farm with cows, we had a young bull with the herd. I asked my brother, "Do you think he'll do anything?"

"Oh, I don't think so," he replied, "he's never tried anything so far."

So with a certain amount of courage, thinking, "Aw, he won't do anything," I walked up to the cows, lying there enjoying the afternoon breeze, so unconcerned, chewing their cuds. They stood up and started lazily for the barn. But the young bull had decided to play a few games with this young country maid. I stood in the very center of the pasture field, face to face with the bull. "What shall I do now?" I thought. I was scared to run, as I knew he could run faster, so I hit him on the head with a dried-up weed, which was the only weapon within reach. Well, he didn't budge. I remembered my grandma saying once that when she was in such a trap she had just flapped her apron, which luckily had frightened the bull into running away. I tried that, but still he did not budge. The next thing I knew, I was going round and round on the ground. That bull must've been having fun! I remembered a story about a man that was in such a trap. He had laid very still, so the bull thought him dead and didn't bother him anymore. So that's what I did; I laid as still and quiet as possible, till the bull had walked a safe distance away, then up I jumped, and never in my life did I run so fast! I didn't look back till I was almost to the fence, and there was the bull coming down the hill, toward me, on a full jump and bellowing. I made it safely across the fence, but in my great fright and excitement, I hadn't even noticed the gash under my left eye until I came to the house and my sister asked what happened.

My parents weren't home. They had gone to a funeral in a neighboring community. So my brother went and told our English neighbors to come with a vehicle. We Amish drive only horses and buggies, and we hire someone with a vehicle only if we need to go a long distance. My brother went with me to where my parents were and brought their horse and buggy home. Then my parents went with me to the nearest hospital. The surgeon there had already put me to sleep when he discovered the injuries were more serious than he had thought. He told us he could have patched my eye shut and risked me losing my eyesight, but he sent us to a bigger hospital where a specialized plastic surgeon did the job. Thanks to the careful surgeon, I still have my eyesight and only a slight scar under my eye. I spent only one week in the hospital. My mom stayed with me all the time and I can say I actually enjoyed it there! I never felt any pain, and I also spent a lot of time in the playroom or brought books back to my room to read.

Since that experience, I have learned never to trust any bull, at any time, no matter how young or timid he may appear. At least that was one time in my life that I was a lucky girl!

Mary Mae Steury
Camden, Michigan

Mama Sent the Rooster Running

Having lived on a farm during my 21 short years of life, I have lots of memories of happenings and accidents. We have always had a coop full of chickens so that we have our own fresh farm eggs. And of course we always have some roosters in the flock too.

One warm forenoon, when I was just a small girl of 3, I was standing by the chicken coop, which is across the driveway from the house. All of a sudden our rooster saw me and must have decided I was just the right size to attack. Up he jumped on top of my head, where he began a pecking and a scratching. Pretty soon I was bleeding, so of course I hollered for my mama, who was up by the house. She came running to my rescue, and it didn't take that old rooster very long to decide to run for cover after seeing Mama's quick slashing hands. I wasn't seriously hurt, just awfully scared!

Barbara M. Graber
Camden, Michigan

I Remember Mama's Geese

Growing up on a Missouri farm in the '20s and '30s gave me many bittersweet memories. Necessities for a big family were not easy to come by. Hard work and ingenuity along with determination kept us going through drought, crop failures, accidents and many childhood diseases. To remember my mama's methods of survival can only make me appreciate more the conveniences that came to me later.

One of her indulgences was a flock of barnyard geese. Not only could she pluck the feathers for our own use, but she delighted in giving feather pillows as gifts and to her own five daughters when they married. Of course we all slept on feather beds. Can you imagine making up feather beds every day, making them smooth and plump? Having geese was something special to her. Once a year when she sold the excess, she had some "mad money." However, she never spent it on herself. The children always needed coats, shoes, overalls and new print dresses.

My dad did not like the geese. They were a nuisance. They chased the baby pigs with their long necks almost to the ground; they dirtied the drinking water. They were such bluffs pretending to scare all the other animals.

Mama always went about her work singing hymns. When the geese heard her coming, they came running to her with squawks and honks. How beautiful they were! I knew what the expression "as big as a goose egg" meant because I gathered the eggs. Each spring they were hatched under an old setting hen because geese built their nests where varmints might get the eggs.

It was my job to catch them when it was time to pluck the feathers. After much squawking and evading me, I would succeed in catching one. Mama would turn it upside down between her knees and pluck the feathers. It must have hurt because the geese protested loudly. Mama would tell me how the outside feathers made the firmness for the pillows and under that was the down that made them soft. After several geese were plucked she had a sackful of feathers to cure until needed. In the wintertime we made the pillows out of heavy ticking, sewing them on the old treadle sewing machine.

After I finished high school, I was determined to go to college. I had worked all summer for the tuition, but in the fall I needed a new winter coat. There was no money, so Mama sold her geese and bought me a coat. It was a huge sacrifice on her part as there were four younger children to send to school. That coat was special!

When I married a few years later, we did get feather pillows for a wedding present. My husband still prefers them to all others.

Auda B. Bratcher
Raytown, Missouri

Don't Squeeze the Chicks

Every spring in the 1930s, my Mother, Mary, would set up an incubator in our living room on the farm to hatch baby chickens. She would light the kerosene lamp that heated the water, which circulated through the incubator. There were pipes throughout the incubator for the warm water to go through.

There were two trays of eggs in the incubator. Each day Mother would pull out the trays and carefully roll the eggs with the palms of her hands. Once a week she would "candle" the eggs. To do this, she would hold each egg up to a special light to see if it was fertile and a chick was developing inside. If not, the egg was destroyed.

After a few weeks, little chicks appeared in the windows of the incubator. When they were dry and fluffy, Mother would "fence" off a corner of the living room with boxes. That was their home until they could go out to the brooder house.

What fun it was to have little baby chicks in the house. But Mother would remind us, "Be careful, don't squeeze them."

Katherine A. Pearson
Siren, Wisconsin

Chapter 4: A Bounty of Good Eating

Nothing Like Homemade Ice Cream

When I was growing up we lived on a farm near Harper, Kansas, and later moved into town, where my father worked for the Santa Fe depot.

My mother's folks lived on a farm near Manchester, Oklahoma, so we went there often as children. A few miles north was Uncle Victor, my dad's brother, and his family. There were three children: two boys and a girl. One of the boys was my age, and the other boy was my brother's age.

We went to Uncle Victor's farm nearly every weekend. They made ice cream with an old-time ice cream freezer that we had to turn by hand. Nothing was as good as that ice cream!

We went to church at the Rosedale Community Church. I was born about one-half mile south of there on December 10, 1911. The church was built with the door in the front part, so that when you came in everybody could see you. You wouldn't dare be late and walk in with everyone watching you! My mom said it was built like that so folks wouldn't have to turn around to see who was coming in.

My father had played a guitar since he was 16 years old, and Uncle Victor played the guitar too, so when we went to Manchester, Dad loaded the guitar in the car, an old Model T sedan, with all of us kids. My mother really got tired of being so crowded in that car.

Grandpa Bennett lived two miles south of Uncle Victor, and he had a high hill out in his pasture. As kids, we would climb to the top of that hill, and on a clear summer day we could see several towns around. One time I rolled halfway down the hill while my dad and uncle were at the foot watching. They just laughed and laughed at the sight, but I didn't think it was so funny.

My grandpa had a big garden each year. The ground was sandy so he raised good tomatoes. Those were the best tomatoes I have ever eaten. We could pick a bucketful in five minutes. Grandma always had a big platter of tomatoes and a platter of fried chicken, roastin' ears and blackberry pie. I ate six roastin' ears one day, besides the chicken and all the rest of the dinner. Grandma said I would sure be sick, but I wasn't.

My brother and I used to go out in the "patch" and eat watermelons. We had a picnic in the yard many times at Grandma's. There was always a big tableful each time we got together. I remember there was always a big bowl of fruit in the center of the table.

We also used to go to another aunt and uncle's north of Harper, Kansas. That uncle had hounds that he used to hunt skunks. He knew I was afraid of dogs, and he would let those hounds out every time I had to go outside to the outhouse.

Once my cousin was there at the same time we were. As we were ironing Grandma's clothes, we came across her underpants. We laughed and laughed because they were long, muslin undies. We had never seen anything like that before!

My uncle, Lee Bennett, had a motorcycle, and as a youngster I rode in the sidecar several times. The road was sandy and he drove a little fast, so we usually went sliding from one side to the other.

As children we used to pick up wheat around the stacks of wheat straw. We got to keep all the wheat we picked up. I almost stepped on a snake while doing that. I found a dime in the house one day, and my sister claimed it was hers. I ran and hid it in the corral for safekeeping, and my father found it months later while working there.

Irene Weed
Fairview, Oklahoma

Dropsy Recipe

This recipe, which is probably from the 1920s, was from my husband's grandmother's collection. It states she received it from Mrs. Will Gray. It calls for equal parts of the following:

cucumber bark (from a cucumber tree)
bark from roots of white ash
silkweed root
one root of ginger, mashed up
one grated nutmeg

Put in one quart of whiskey or Jamaican rum. Take one teaspoonful three times a day. If too strong lessen the dose. Take enough to have a bowel movement three or four times a day. A handful of "eack" bark can be substituted for the silkweed.

Grandmother Valeria Younger Schofield lived to be almost 90; she was a "teetotaler." She died in 1967 and I remember she loved to guzzle down those big bottles of Coca-Cola in her old age with no stomach problems. Those old-timers were made of good stuff, not like the whiners of today.

Mary Lu Beemer Schofield
Lenox, Iowa

Food From the Land

The life of a farmer in the 1930s was a demanding one, revolving around the seasons. Most of our food was grown on the land. Staples, such as flour, sugar, salt, soap, etcetera, were bought in Rochester. We often traded eggs for these items.

Chickens supplied not only eggs but much of our meat. Sunday dinners and other special meals usually featured chicken in some form. The chicken might be fried, roasted, or boiled with homemade noodles. Sometimes a hog or calf was butchered in the late fall. It was possible to preserve meat in a variety of ways—it could be canned, smoked or salted. We were especially fond of canned veal. During hunting season Dad shot rabbits, ducks and an occasional pheasant to supplement our meat supply. Sometimes he even killed a large turtle, which is considered a delicacy—it tastes like chicken. However, I never liked to eat it, as I could not banish the unpleasant image of the turtle from my mind.

We kept a herd of dairy cattle when we lived at Polk's Hill. During the spring and summer Dad put them in a far pasture that he referred to as "the west 40." My sister and I had the job of going to the field in the late afternoon to drive the cows home for milking. To reach this pasture we walked down a winding lane, past two ponds, through the woods, and out into a sunlit field. Many things caught our interest along the way. In the spring we looked for mushrooms or picked wild flowers. We usually left home a little earlier than necessary, so we would have time to swing on a sturdy wild grapevine that hung from a large tree at the edge of the path. Bowser, a tan-and-white mixed-breed dog, ran ahead of us, inspecting all of the rustling noises in the leaves covering the lane. I wish I could say that she was a great help in rounding up the cows, but she was not a working dog. We knew each of the cows and called them by name—Red, Tiny, Bess, Lady, etc. The cows were all gentle creatures and moved obediently along the path toward the barn.

My parents did all of the milking by hand. The milk was poured into 10-gallon cans, which were picked up daily and taken to the Armour Creamery in Rochester. At times we sold cream instead of milk. The milk was put into a machine called a separator, which was operated by turning a handle. The cream was taken to the creamery and the skimmed milk was fed to the hogs. We used raw milk for cooking, drinking and churning butter from sour cream.

We had a large garden and an even larger truck patch. Gooseberry, strawberry, blackberry, rhubarb and asparagus plants grew along the boundaries of the garden. An orchard supplied a variety of apples and plums. An old cherry tree stood in the corner of the yard and produced abundantly each summer. An equally old pear tree also continued to produce small, hard pears that littered the yard each fall. A grape arbor was planted beyond the orchard and truck patch. Mom canned quarts of grape juice, which she used to make jelly and grape pies. Dad bought a grape press and tried, unsuccessfully, to make wine. Wild black raspberries grew in one of the woods on the farm. We loved fresh, sugared raspberries with cream poured over them. Another of our favorite desserts was warm raspberry dumplings.

The entire family was kept busy from early spring, when the seeds were planted, until fall, when the harvest was brought in. Even the children helped in planting seeds, pulling weeds, picking vegetables and cleaning them. The entire summer was spent in preparation for the coming winter, with endless picking, cleaning and canning of fruits and vegetables. When farm wives met they took great pride in telling each other how many jars of each fruit and vegetable they had put up.

In the fall or winter Dad worked in the woods, clearing out dead trees to be used as firewood. Sometimes he found a hollow "bee tree" and carried the honeycombs home in a washtub. The honey was boiled on the stove to sterilize it, then strained and poured into glass jars. It provided a welcome change from molasses. Maple trees supplied another kind of syrup. In the early spring Dad drilled a hole in the trunk of the tree and hung a bucket on a nail to catch the sap as it ran out. This sap, which tasted like sweet water, was strained and boiled down to syrup. Due to evaporation during boiling, it took a large amount of sap to make a small amount of syrup.

The woods also gave us black walnuts in the fall and morel mushrooms in the spring. Certain areas in the catalpa groves provided ideal growing conditions for these sponge mushrooms. Dad knew all of the places in which to search. He had an eagle eye that could spot a mushroom when no one else could see it. He often went mushroom hunting the first thing in the morning before the rest of the family had awakened. While he milked the cows, Mom cleaned and fried mushrooms. If the yield was not plentiful that morning, scrambled eggs were added in order to stretch the mushrooms. Regardless of the method of preparation, we thought that was the best breakfast in the world.

One of the dangers of mushroom hunting was the possibility of meeting a snake in the woods. For this reason we were reluctant to go into the woods alone. Blue racer snakes were often seen in the woods where the mushrooms grew. When Dad was with us we felt safe, as we knew he would protect us by killing any snakes that appeared. He warned us that we should never make sudden movements around snakes, but should back away quietly. We had an opportunity to test this advice one day when we children were alone in the woods looking for mushrooms. Hearing a strange rattling sound, I looked toward the noise and saw a coiled snake a few feet away. The gray and black diamond pattern of the snake blended into the surrounding leaf-covered ground. Had it not been for the warning the snake gave us, we might have walked right into its path. The head was extended toward us with the tongue darting out. Remembering Dad's advice we cautiously and quietly backed away. This took a certain amount of will power, as our natural inclination was to run as fast as we could. That is exactly what we did—when we were a safe distance away from the snake!

Although I loved living on the hill, at times I envied town children who had playmates in their neighborhoods and sidewalks to skate on. In contrast, my husband, who grew up in a city, envied country people. When he visited relatives in Wisconsin, he was only aware of the rich and plentiful food that was heaped on their plates. He knew nothing of the hours of labor involved in producing that food. Despite the fact that we all had to do our share of the work and had no money for luxuries, the land fed us at a time when many people were hungry. We were among the fortunate.

Barbara L. Hintz
Overland Park, Kansas

Food Tasted Better Back Then

What a life! Childhood on a farm with my parents and three sisters. Our whole social life centered around the family. School was the highlight of our life. Summer was a time of dreaming, reading and long walks in the pasture.

The evenings were always spent singing. In the winter Mother played the piano and we all sang. Dad also taught us to square dance. In the summer we sat on the front porch, since it was before the days of air conditioning. Then Mother would play the guitar. How we loved all the old cowboy songs and hymns!

I remember the huge garden and the hours of canning produce, the cows to milk twice a day, and the chicken coop full of fryers and layers. Mother would chop the heads off with a hatchet—how good they tasted at noon.

I especially remember the first fried chicken and homemade ice cream on the Fourth of July. Why doesn't food taste that good anymore?

Rose M. Fehr
Sutton, Nebraska

The Secret Meat Loaf

When I was a small girl my mother could not drink cow's milk as it made her ill, so Dad bought some goats.

With a 12-foot fence, he doubled-fenced a small yard to keep the goats inside. One night he parked his Ford nearby. It had a tarpaper top. The next morning Dad found those goats had jumped from the yard, over the 12-foot fence and landed with all four feet through his car top. I've never seen my dad quite as angry as he was that day!

We also butchered the goats for meat. It was delicious when Mom fried it, and she made good meat loaf. But many neighbors said they wouldn't eat goats' meat. "No, Sir." One night at a school PTA supper she took the meat loaf. It was the only meat we had! She enjoyed hearing the comments on her delicious meat loaf. People were going back for seconds and telling their friends to try it. Mother's meat loaf disappeared fast, and she never told anyone they were eating goats' meat.

Gloria Williams
Grandview, Missouri

Childhood Memories

I have many wonderful memories of an 800-acre farm in southeast Kansas where I was born and lived until I married. I was an only child until I was almost 7 years old.

Our nearest neighbor was nearly a mile away by way the crow flies, so I didn't often have playmates. I learned to amuse myself. I always had a favorite cat. I learned early to ride in front of my dad in the saddle. Our transportation then was horseback or buggy. We attended a country church about four miles away. We made the 10-mile trip to town every week or two. A trip took most of the day. Mama sold cream, butter, eggs, chickens and garden produce.

I learned at an early age to help with the farm chores. I disliked churning because it seemed the cream was either too cold or too warm to become butter quickly. I liked cattle and sometimes had a pet calf. When one of the milk cows had a calf I decided to pet him, but the cow didn't want my affection. She gently pushed me between her horns against the barn and held me away from the calf. I was a brave 4-year-old and just talked to Bossy until she let me go. I made "beautiful" mud pies, cakes and sculptures. I had lots of cousins, and families visited occasionally, but all were several miles away. I walked a mile to a one-room school of a dozen or more pupils. One day my fellow first grader and I whispered too much and the teacher made Warren and me sit together. How awful!

One January morning when I got up, I saw the doctor at the house. Dad said I had a baby brother. I was so pleased I didn't want to go to school. It was fun to help take care of him. The next six years added another brother and two sisters to our family. Mama was then very busy. She no longer helped in the hay making. Dad thought I was big enough to drive a team, so I helped mow, rake and buck hay. It was fun unless a snake slithered out of the hay. One day I raked over a bumblebee nest. The horses got stung and we made some crazy windrows before I got them settled down. I learned to milk and take care of the chickens.

Mama always raised a big garden. We canned or dried all sorts of vegetables and what fruit we could get. The dried corn was especially good. I knew the location of every wild plum, grape and gooseberry on that ranch. Mama sometimes made pumpkin butter, which is almost like apple butter. Dad dried cured pork. Sometimes we would fry sausage and pack it in lard in a stone jar or crock. We had no refrigeration, but the lard method worked well in cold winter weather. Sometimes Dad killed a wild duck or rabbit and caught fish. Mother was a resourceful cook and made good nourishing meals. Sometimes we had corn meal mush and milk with a spoonful of molasses or vegetable soup for supper on cold winter nights. No bakery bread can compare in aroma or flavor to Mama's bread. If we were hungry when we came home from school, she might cut the crust from a warm loaf, butter the end of the loaf, then cut off the buttered slice for us.

My friend Isla and I helped our dads with cattle. We had to drive them to the railroad 10 miles away to send them to the Kansas City market. Sometimes we would run races—she on Buddy and I on Daisy. I can't think of a prettier sight than looking out on a sunny, dewy, early morning and seeing cows and calves on the pasture slope near our house. The pasture sparkled like diamonds. A white-faced calf might give a gentle bawl as he scampered to get his breakfast, and the cow would answer in a soft moo. Other cattle pairs dotted the hillside. It was a beautiful picture of contentment.

This story sounds like all we did was work. We not only worked together, we fished, picnicked, went to town and visited family and friends.

I have enough memories of that ranch to fill a book, such as our first car, the new house, Mama's illness, growing up with brothers and sisters, different animals, storms and much more. A niece and I now own the ranch, which my dad bought in about 1907. It is all pasture now and is used for grazing.

Mary Worley
Azalea, Oregon

Learning How to Cook

I was raised in Houston, Texas. I finished my last year of high school in Louisiana and met my husband in Shreveport. He was from a small farming area about 40 miles north of Birmingham, Alabama, and lived on a farm.

When we married he took me to the farm. After 49 years farming is in my blood. We have a huge garden to share with our three married children and their families, as well as our neighbors.

We have a lot of laughs now about our early farming days. We bought 53 acres and grew corn and cotton. One year Ed said if we could pick the cotton ourselves we'd have more money to pay on our land. Boy! Was he surprised! I really had to work hard to pick 100 pounds of cotton in one day. He never had to pick cotton at home so it was all he could do to pick 100 pounds himself. When we got our first bale he said he'd better find someone to help us because if it started raining we could lose our crop. My cotton was very clean because I picked the burrs and leaves out of it before putting any in my sack. Everyone tried to tell me the ginning would clean it. I still picked through it.

Ed taught me to cook all those wonderful vegetables. I'm lucky to still have him. A neighbor gave me some hot peppers and I tried to cook some soup. Ed told me I could put a little in the soup, so I cut up four or five big, long pods in my pot. It looked so good. Ed took a bite for supper and grabbed his glass of milk. I asked what was wrong and he said the soup was hot. I thought he meant from boiling, but it was so peppery we couldn't eat it. I was determined to fix it, so I added vegetables to it every day for four or five days, but it never was edible. The more I cooked it the hotter it got.

When my father was coming out for a visit Ed brought a 12-quart basket of eggs. I had never seen so many eggs in my life. I scrambled 12 eggs for breakfast for the three of us. Needless to say most of them were thrown out.

When Ed's father was going to eat with us one day, Ed asked me to cook some turnips and greens. I really scrubbed those turnips. Ed passed them to Mr. Blackwood and he dipped out a spoonful.

The turnip roots were hanging off the side of the spoon. I tried to explain how I really tried to scrub them with a brush. They didn't eat them. The next day I tried to fry squash. Well I was going to do them right so I peeled them. I thought if you peeled the turnips you must also peel the squash, but I was wrong; they just mashed up when I tried to fry them.

I learned to milk our cow, and at one time we were milking a black cow. A friend's son came down from Gasden and spent a week with us. He came out to the barn while I was milking the black cow and told me, "Now I know where chocolate milk comes from."

Ed's mother told me one time I'd never know how she tried to find something to cook that I would eat. I liked sandwiches, and if Ed had not taken me to the cafe every afternoon I don't guess I would have survived. That cafe made the best chicken salad sandwiches. I did learn to eat vegetables since I had to cook them for Ed.

I really had to learn a lot about farming but I wouldn't take anything for those experiences in our early years. Farming is hard work but I wouldn't trade living on the farm for any city life.

Peggy Blackwood
Cleveland, Alabama

Mother's Plentiful Garden

My mind goes back to the early '50s when I grew up on a small farm in Iowa. We were struggling to make the payments on our farm, so my parents had to think of ways to cut expenses. One thing my mother did was to raise a garden. At first my mother planted what she thought was just enough for our needs. Invariably, it seemed something always happened to the crop. Either somebody stole it the night before she planned to harvest it, or bad weather or insects wiped it out. After several years of this, my mother finally decided the Lord must be trying to tell her something. The next year she planted more than she thought we needed. We had a bumper crop. Then my mother started thinking about all the people who didn't have gardens or those who had less money than we did. She began giving away the abundance and found great joy in seeing people's eyes light up. Every year after that we had huge gardens. We always had more than enough. I'm so glad my mother taught me the valuable lessons of generosity and compassion.

Joy J. Palmer
Forest City, Iowa

Mother's Wonderful Cooking

I have so many memories of my youth and the life we lived on the farm, I hardly know where to start. There were nine of us kids, so we were always cooking and washing dishes. In winter, when a cow and hog were butchered, we rendered lard in a big copper boiler on the wood cookstove. Mom would stir it with the long wooden ladle that was used to churn butter in the tall crock churn. Apple butter was also made in this old copper boiler, and wash water was heated in it too.

In early spring Mom would get baby chicks, possibly 200 or so. She would get up in the night and go out to the brooder house to check on them and add wood to the heater. These chickens would be our meat supply for summer, as we had no way to keep meat. Later on in the summer more chicks would be raised for fryers.

We had no electricity, but we had the kerosene lamps, the wood cookstove and heaters. I recall in winter how the dipper in the water bucket would freeze in the water. In summer as well as in winter we ate in the kitchen by the big wood cookstove. I don't recall anyone ever complaining about how hot it was, as we knew nothing else.

Mom was a wonderful cook, using lots of cream, butter and sugar. Most every night for supper we had a huge skillet of fried potatoes; to this day I still love them. We baked bread every other day in big, black bread pans that were my grandfather's when he batched; he was 40 when he married Grandma, who was 20. These pans were so worn that there were tiny holes in the bottom.

On the Fourth of July we would get ice! What a treat. We would have a big freezer of ice cream, and Mom would make orangeade from real oranges and lemons. This was made in a five-gallon stone jar with a big hunk of ice in it. This stone jar sat on the floor by Mom. The empty glasses were passed down the row of kids to Mom, who would refill them and pass them back up the row. We sat on long boards that rested on five-gallon cream cans.

Though it sounds as if we lived a hard life, it did not seem so to us, as it was all we knew.

Lena M. Wyrick
Waverly, Kansas

Home-Grown Sunday Dinners

I have always liked gardening, as we all know it is hard but satisfying work. We always had a big garden because we were a big family. We also raised chickens and had a milk cow. The chickens gave us eggs and meat and the cow gave us milk and butter. We also had a timber lot behind the house with a cherry tree in it.

I think my mother was one of the best cooks a kid could have. One of my favorite meals was at harvesting time. Mom would kill a couple of chickens and fry them for Sunday dinner. She could make the best creamed peas with new potatoes and onions —nobody could match her sauce. We would have fried new wilted lettuce, green beans and anything else we had in the garden. The bread was made from scratch and the butter was also homemade. For dessert Mom would make cherry pie.

Near the end of the summer, we had grown or raised everything on the table ourselves. Mom was such a good cook that many times people would drop in on Sunday and eat with us. Somehow Mom always had enough to go around. I never knew of anyone being turned away even in the toughest of times.

Janice Gatlin
Osawatomie, Kansas

A Cornucopia of Food

On the farm, food for the family was mostly home grown and preserved by the farm wife. The garden was started as soon as the ground dried out and warmed up a bit; it had been plowed the fall before. The potatoes were the first thing in the ground. Eyes were taken from sprouted potatoes in the bin in the cave, or later we purchased seed potatoes in 100-pound gunnysacks. Radishes, onions, lettuce, peas, beets, carrots and spinach were planted for early crops too. It wouldn't be long until the ground warmed up and the little weeds started making their appearance. Out came the hoe to keep them under control—no motor-powered tillers in those days. Later the corn was planted when the hedge leaves were the size of squirrels ears. Beans, cabbage, green peppers, tomatoes, pumpkins, squash, cucumbers, sweet potatoes and melons were planted when there was no longer a chance of frost. Turnips were sown the 25th of July, wet or dry.

The first green onions, radishes and lettuce were the very best tasting. Our summer meals consisted mainly of the garden produce that happened to be ready at the time. The job of canning and preserving for winter was just beginning. You canned everything that you didn't eat fresh, as your summer work was the basis of most of your winter meals. Somewhere along the line I read a saying, "Eat what you can and can what you can't." I don't remember a time my mother didn't have a pressure canner, but before she did she "hot-water bathed" peas, beans and corn for several hours on a wood stove in the wash house. Thank goodness for the wash house as our house would have been a steamy tomb to try to sleep in at night with no fans or air conditioner.

Cucumbers became sweet, dill and bread-and-butter pickles; cabbage became kraut; tomatoes were juiced and whole tomatoes were canned for winter vegetable soup and chili. Fall brought time to dig the potatoes; Dad dug and the kids picked them up. After they were sorted they were stored in the "tater bin" in the cave for the winter. We always kept out the smallest ones to use first, as they would soon shrivel and be almost impossible to peel.

There was always a big strawberry patch. Along with the berries came the job of standing on your head in the hot June sunshine, picking them every couple of days as long as the season lasted. Despite the hard work of pulling and hoeing the weeds, we enjoyed many meals of fresh strawberry shortcake or just strawberries and cream. Strawberry jam was also put up for the winter; some berries were canned for fruit sauce but they never had the taste of fresh ones. There was an apple tree for fresh and canned applesauce and spicy apple butter. Fall apples were stored in the cave in boxes for winter use, along with buckets of carrots and turnips and beets, which were stored in damp sand. There were also pumpkins and squash for pies.

When the old hens quit laying and the spring pullets were put in the laying house, the old hens were killed and dressed and canned for chicken and noodles, cream chicken and biscuits or hot chicken sandwiches. If the beef was butchered some of it was also canned for later use—nothing tastes like home-canned beef.

We picked blackberries, wild raspberries and gooseberries in the timber and along the fence rows. Most of these were eaten fresh or in pies; if they were really plentiful some were canned or made into jelly. A trip to the timber with a picnic lunch to gather walnuts and hickory nuts was a fun outing for the whole family on crisp fall days. The trip supplied the nuts for creamy fudge or spicy homemade oatmeal cookies or anything else you would chock full of nuts for more flavor.

During the summer when you were preserving for the winter, there were weeds in the garden to keep under control, the usual meals to prepare, laundry, cooking for hired hands, ironing and taking care of the kids. By doing all of this work, the wife helped out with the family farm.

Ann Wyer
Corydon, Iowa

Chapter 5: Harvesting and Hard Work

Milking the Cows

We kids were probably around 9 years old. We did the chore of milking the cows. One Sunday evening we went to visit some friends who had kids about our age. They were still doing their chores, so we helped them. There were enough cows for each of us to have one to milk. There were several cats around so we tried to see who could squirt the milk the farthest into the cats' mouths. They loved it and so did we.

We soon tired of that and discovered a new type of contest. There were lots of flies so we began to pop them off into the milk buckets to see who could catch the most! Our moms were not too pleased with this idea and we were severely reprimanded. Our milk was poured out for the pigs. I never tried that game again!

I had a large pair of white coveralls that we wore at school as the pep squad at the football games. Mine were extra large so they couldn't shrink too small and so I could put lots of clothes under them when it was real cold. I hurried to milk my cow so I could go to the game. There were lots of flies, and the cow was stomping them off her legs when somehow she inserted her foot into the left hip pocket of my coveralls. It knocked me off my one-legged stool, which overturned the bucket of milk onto me. I was a mess! I didn't go to the game as my coveralls and I had to be washed. My dignity had been squashed!

I loved to read and would do it at any opportunity I could find. I thought it took lots of time to milk a cow so I combined it with reading. I couldn't quite get a book to prop up right on my left leg, but a magazine I could manage okay. I had to milk early though, while there was still light to read by.

My mother had a saying, "If you don't learn to milk a cow, you won't have to," and she didn't, but often my brother or father was harvesting late and someone had to do it. Since she couldn't—I had to!

Gloria Williams
Grandview, Missouri

Picking Gooseberries

Yes, I said gooseberries, those little green, sour obnoxious wild berries that grew abundantly in our timber. How in the world did our mother get us to go there day after day with a bucket on our arm and a determined look on our faces? The bushes were found among poison ivy, snakes, mosquitoes, gnats and prickly under-brush. We picked until they were all gone because in those days we never let anything go to waste. Actually, they were kind of good saturated with sugar over hot biscuits and covered with good thick cream.

Every year as soon as school was out in May, it was time to pick gooseberries. If she could, Mom would go with us and keep telling us how she enjoyed being out of doors away from the old cookstove. She couldn't stay away very long because duty called her to get that all important noon meal for our big family of nine. My two younger sisters and I toiled away trying to get a gallon bucket full before noon. If we were lucky and found an unpicked patch, we could go home at noon with a bucketful.

Could we then wash them as we did strawberries and eat them? No siree! They had to be stemmed one by one. Two sides of each berry had to be plucked with your fingernail. This was worse than the picking to active children like us. Sometimes Mom had one of our grandmothers come to help her stem. They could sit on the front porch and visit while they worked, and they didn't seem to mind at all.

Believe it or not there were people in town who would buy them. This gave us incentive to pick until we dropped. One older lady must have liked them very much. She would call and order a gallon or two. We charged 25 cents per gallon. In those days a quarter was big money to a country kid. So we took our gallon buckets and picked them full, savoring those quarters. I remember knocking on her back door with two bucketfuls. Delighted, she invited us in and took them to her kitchen table where she proceeded to pour them into a gallon crock. I remember my anxiety as she heaped them up above the rim. Two gallons became one and one-half gallons and I had to divide the profits with my sister. I really squawked when I got home, and we laugh about it to this day. I guess it was one of life's hard knocks.

June was usually a miserable month for me because I was one that got poison ivy, and there was no relief for it then. I can remember my legs being a solid mass of blisters and scratches from the briers. Why didn't someone tell me what poison ivy looked like so I could avoid it?

As I grew older I rebelled and opted to stay at the house and do the ironing or get dinner. I wonder what kids would do in 1995 if confronted with such a task? I might say "try it you'll like it," but they wouldn't like it. Memories are such pleasures when one gets old!

Auda B. Bratcher
Raytown, Missouri

Dividing the Chores

Every member of our farm family of six children had chores to do either inside or outside. Since I was in the middle age-wise I thought I got the jobs no one else wanted—the others probably thought that too. Typical chores for me, a child in the 1930s and '40s, included carrying pails of water to the house for general use. Since there was no running water it all needed to be carried and everyone helped with this chore. The reservoir on the side of the kitchen range needed to be filled so there would be warm water for cooking, washing dishes or bathing, and the big teakettle that took its place on the back side of the range for extra hot water always needed to be filled, as did the drinking water pail.

Feeding the flock of laying hens and gathering their eggs was another chore—not one I especially liked, but chickens were an important part of the family food supply. It was an exciting day in the spring when the baby chicks arrived, either by our own pick-up service from a local hatchery, or by mail, when the rural mail carrier delivered them from an order sent to a distant hatchery. The little balls of yellow fluff were cute for about two days, and then they sprouted feathers and required more care, feed, water and litter changing. There was always the fear of dreaded coccidiosis, which could take the lives of dozens of baby chicks a day. When the young chickens became 3 to 4 months old the roosters were dressed for fryers and the pullets were saved to lay eggs the next year. The old hens that were past egg-laying were dressed, canned for chicken and noodles or dumplings or sold. The eggs were gathered daily during warm weather, and several times a day during the cold winter months to prevent freezing.

In the spring there were always hens that developed the mothering instinct and were "sitters"—they quit laying eggs, and just sat on the nest hoping to hatch a bunch of chicks. Since the eggs were gathered daily, they didn't get to sit on them and tend them the three weeks it took to hatch a baby chick. Nevertheless, they would continue to sit on that nest unless they were shut up in a coop to break the habit. They became very crabby while setting and would peck your hand or arm when you attempted to retrieve the eggs from beneath them. Eggs were used in many ways on the menu of farm families. The eggs that weren't consumed were taken to the local produce station that bought our cream and eggs. The cream and egg money was what the housewife had to purchase her groceries with. If there was any left over, there might be a new "something" for the house or a new pair of shoes for someone.

Our lighting system consisted of kerosene lamps, which I filled with kerosene two or three times a week along with cleaning and polishing their chimneys. Newspapers were used to help remove the black soot and give them a shine. Later we were blessed with the Aladdin lamp, which had a mantle rather than a wick to burn—it gave a much brighter light.

Milking cows and feeding hogs were other daily chores that I didn't do on a regular basis but helped with when needed, especially in summer months when the men were busy with fieldwork.

Shocking oats was a seasonal chore that was awful. The oats were cut and tied into bundles with a machine and left lying on the ground. Then a crew came along to "shock" the bundles by standing them up tepee style so the grain would dry and could be threshed by the threshing crew later. I helped with the shocking for a few years as I became old enough to endure that hot, scratchy job.

Most of the household chores were taken care of by my two older sisters, so I didn't really become efficient at housework. Ironing dishtowels, handkerchiefs and pillowcases seemed to fall to me because they were easy and there were plenty of shirts, blouses and dresses to be ironed by those more talented.

"Leading the hay horse" was another chore I acquired as I grew adept enough to keep ahead of the horse. Before we had bales of hay, the hay was brought in from the field loose on a hayrack and parked in front of the barn. A huge hay fork on a pulley was secured into a "bite" of hay. The pulley was attached to a large rope running up and across the roof, inside the barn and out the other side, where it was hooked to the harness on the hay horse. When the signal was given, the hay horse leader led the horse, pulling the fork of hay up into the barn until someone gave the signal to stop. Then they pulled the rope releasing the hay into the haymow. You always hoped you could keep ahead of the horse so he didn't step on your heels with his big hooves!

Margaret Blair
Lorimor, Iowa

The Best Childhood is on a Farm

My parents farmed 80 acres in Cushing, Wisconsin. I was born in 1922; a doctor and a midwife delivered me at the farmhouse. I lived through the Depression, when money was scarce to make the mortgage payments. The man who received the mortgage payments said, "If you can't pay on the principal, just be sure you keep up the interest payments." Sometimes Dad would have to ship a calf south to St. Paul to get a little money.

The farm became my playground. When the wild blackberries, strawberries, raspberries and gooseberries ripened in the woods I fastened a small pail on my belt and picked them. Wild plums, chokecherries and pincherries grew along the fence line. Mom made jelly from those. In order to pick them, I drove an old gentle mare hitched to the buggy. She ate grass while I stood in the buggy to reach the fruit.

Early in my life I rode horseback on one of the work horses while Dad plowed or cultivated. I hung onto the harness. Dad let me ride his saddle horse at age 5, and from then until I left home at 19 I rode horseback nearly every day except in the winter. Mom got a trifle exasperated with me because she needed help in the house. Pails of water had to be brought from the well, and wood from the woodshed. If she'd ask me to wash the supper dishes, I'd say, "Yeah, but I just want to go for a little ride first."

We didn't have electricity until about 1928. Before that, with no refrigeration, perishables had to be taken to the cellar between meals. With no electric washing machine, Mom scrubbed clothes on a washboard and boiled them in a boiler on the wood-burning cookstove. The ironing was done with sad-irons that were heated on the stove—very heavy, usually too hot—which scorched the clothes or were not hot enough. Kerosene lamps provided light at night, and a lantern was carried from the house to the barn.

My grandparents, Sheldon and Mary Armstrong, had homesteaded the land in 1875. Their six sons and one daughter grew up there. My dad, Ray Armstrong, continued to farm with his dad when he got home from France after World War I. Grandma died in 1921, so when Dad and Mother married they bought the farm, while Grandpa continued to live there. What a lucky arrangement for me, as I tagged along with Grandpa; I learned all about farming from him. He became frail and was hospitalized with kidney stones—he died before I was ready for such a calamity.

Dad continually cleared more land. He cut down trees for wood and hauled rocks to a ravine. With the team and sled in the winter he hauled cordwood to St. Croix Falls, 12 miles away. He was so proud of his team; they'd pull anything. Once he hitched the team to the school bus and pulled it out of the mud when it was stuck on the road.

Numerous family reunions took place at our house, especially on July Fourth. Eager cousins took turns cranking the two-gallon ice cream freezer. Uncle Ernest had an icehouse so he brought the chunk of ice. He cut ice each winter and kept the chunks between layers of sawdust in the icehouse. They had an icebox in their kitchen—a "modern appliance"—before electricity, so they needed ice. Sometimes the men pitched horseshoes while they waited for dinner.

Mom handled these large gatherings very capably. She always had a large garden; the cellar shelves were loaded with canned fruits, vegetables, pickles and relishes. Every time Uncle Frank came she opened a jar of watermelon pickles—his favorite. A few young roosters became the meat for dinner, they'd been tiny chicks in the brooder house only a few months before. Mom usually served creamed new potatoes with peas from the garden on the Fourth. The potatoes were small, yet everyone raved over that dish.

Dad never had a tractor, but since his death in 1964 my brother, Ken Armstrong, has farmed the Armstrong homestead. He doesn't have horses. I've often thought what a different kind of life his daughters have had growing up on that same farm. They never knew the house when it didn't have a bathroom, running water or a furnace. I wonder now why I didn't freeze going to the outhouse on below zero days.

Lucille Anton
Circle Pines, Minnesota

The Sugar Beet Story

Sugar beets have been a farm crop for many years, and through the years there have been many changes in their planting, thinning and harvesting.

The first sugar beet seeds literally exploded when planted, causing one seed to produce up to 15 little beet plants. Since there should be only one beet in about 10 to 12 inches of space, it was necessary to thin the beets. One person would block with the hoe, and the next person would crawl behind and from the clump pull out all beets except one. This, of course, was a very tedious job that required many hours of work.

In time, through experimentation, a segmented seed was developed, preventing so many beets from developing from one seed. Mechanical thinners also became popular for eliminating the extra beets in the row. We had a "Blackwelder" thinner that my husband simply attached to the back of the tractor. It was a device that covered about a two-inch clump of beets, cutting out about eight inches of other beets. We then followed in the row with a hoe, and removed all beets except one plant from this clump. At that time my children, along with some of their friends, and I thinned about 50 acres of beets in a year.

We now have what is called a mono-germ sugar beet seed. This means that only one plant comes up from one seed. Now the sugar beets are space planted, and the hand labor of thinning beets is completely eliminated.

When the farmer plants the beet seed, he also sprays herbicides in an eight- to 10-inch band on the beet row. In ideal weather conditions, the spray literally eliminates all weeds from coming up in the sugar beet row, again saving the hand labor of weeding the beets with a hoe. However, the beets need to be cultivated several times during the growing season to prevent the weeds from growing between the rows, which could literally choke the growing sugar beet. Ideally, the beets are planted in early April, but there are times when weather doesn't permit the farmer to do any planting until late May.

Beets were originally harvested by hand, but in the early '40s, a mechanical beet harvester that was pulled by a tractor appeared on the scene. This harvested one or two rows of beets at one time. Defoliators, which beat the leaves off the beets before the harvester came along and lifted the beets out of the ground, were also invented.

A good sugar beet yield is 25 tons of beets per acre, with a sugar content of 17-18 percent per acre. When the sugar beets are taken to the processing plant, the loaded truck is weighed, then proceeds to a beet piler. About five beets are taken from various parts of the truckload, and these are tested for sugar content. The beets are then unloaded from the truck, the dirt that has been shaken from the beets is loaded onto the farmer's truck, and he again crosses the scales. The weight of the empty truck is then deducted from the weight of the full truck, and the remaining number is the actual tons of beets that were brought in on that truck.

When the beets reach the processing plant, they are washed, sliced, and placed in a very large cooker. After the appropriate length of cooking time, they go into a spinning process whereby the sugar gets spun away from the beet pulp and comes out of the cooker as fine grains of white sugar.

Besides granulated white sugar, there are also sugar beet by-products, namely beet pulp and molasses. These by-products are utilized as cattle feed.

The sugar beet campaign starts in October when the first loads of beets arrive at the factory, and lasts until the very last beet has been taken from the very last pile—usually in February.

Grace Roedel
Frankenmuth, Michigan

Threshing Meant Work, Fun and Fellowship

Threshing time was an exciting time to be around. The evening before your wheat or oats were to be threshed, the big machine would pull into your place in order to be ready to go early in the morning. Everyone hoped it wouldn't rain.

To us it meant someone would be picked to take the jugs of water to the men in the field, and they would be paid to do it. It was fun to watch the neighbor women coming in to help my mother cook for the men who came to help and the threshing crew. The next day, she would go help one of the other neighbors.

The day before they would start baking bread, pies, cakes and anything else they could fix ahead of time. A lot of talking and laughing went into preparing that meal. Long tables were set up. Wash basins were put on benches outside for the men to wash up before dinner. At noon the dinner bell, if you had one, would ring.

We couldn't believe how much the men could eat. As young children, we hoped some would be left for us. If the men were running late with the threshing, they might also be there for supper.

By afternoon, the women would have the kitchen clean and were deciding what the neighbor would be serving the next day. They would try to think up a variety of different foods. With no refrigerator it was hard to fix too much ahead.

The farmers who were having the dinner would drive into town for chunks of ice from the icehouse. These would help keep food cold and provide ice for the cold drinks. Can you imagine how tired everyone was, doing everything the hard way?

It was always a relief to have your grain threshed before rain ruined your crops. Selling that grain meant you would have money to live on that year and the next. We had a lot of hard work, but we always had fun too.

Today a lot of farmers have their own combines and don't need a crew. The wife of the farmer might get a meal ready with her electric stove and her refrigerator. She might have an air conditioner to keep her cool and a dishwasher to do her dishes. Instead of the grain being hauled into town on wagons, a truck will take it in just as it is being combined. There is less work today, but there is also less fellowship. The children miss out on the fun.

Mildred Swinford
Keokuk, Iowa

The Runaway Tractor

Stories about farm tractors always remind me of our 9-year-old sister, Missy, and her visit to the family farm in Virginia more than half a century ago.

It was midday and everyone was sitting around the lunch table, relaxing before resuming a never-ending round of farm chores. Suddenly, the sounds of a tractor being activated wafted through the air, causing a momentary silence at the table.

Uncle Ben exclaimed, "What the Sam Hill?" as he jumped from his seat and ran toward the back porch—Sam Hill was as close to cussing as he ever came—with the rest of the clan close behind.

Across the field the tractor was beginning to move. "Who the Sam Hill is up there?" Uncle Ben shouted, while racing for the spot where the machine was now randomly working its way.

Reaching his goal, he leapt up and, with one motion of his hand, brought the tractor to a halt. Then he came down with a smiling Missy under his arm.

In due time, the excitement died out and farm life returned to normal, with Uncle Ben on the tractor and everyone else following Aunt Bessie's advice to "Keep out of his way until he cools off!"

Missy never could explain exactly how she started that machine; nor could she understand what the commotion was all about. After all, as she said, "I just wanted to help Uncle Ben."

Later that summer Uncle Ben, who must have harbored a secret admiration for such enterprising behavior on the part of a tiny girl, began teaching Missy the rudiments of driving. Two years later, having promised to avoid tractors, Missy was driving the old Model T—or was it a Model A ?—around the farm. When her envious peers were not feeding the chickens or performing some other mundane activity they were confined to bareback riding on a passive old mare.

Bill Riola
Lakewood, New Jersey

An Old-Fashioned Threshing Bee

Many communities today schedule old-fashioned threshing bees so the younger generation can see how oats were harvested in bygone days.

In the "good old days" of 50 or so years ago the threshing crew was called a "ring," because it made a circuit of a number of farms. Each farmer furnished labor, and in order to get the necessary number of men, those having more acres of oats to be threshed had to furnish two men, or in a few cases, three men with teams of horses and racks.

There were bundle haulers, who loaded the oat shocks onto a rack, hauled them to the threshing machine, then pitched them into the machine. The grain haulers had to take care of the threshed grain. Some farmers had elevators to unload the grain; others did not, so the oats had to be put into the granary with the scoop shovel method. Many nights after the chores were done (and darkness had descended) my dad would scoop off at least one load of grain.

Some of the farmers stacked the straw, so a good stacker was always in demand. His job was extremely dirty and hot. All day he worked in the straw stack, arranging it neatly so it would stay in place. At other farms the straw was left in a pile as it came from the blower. There always seemed to be a bit of prestige involved if you had a straw stack instead of just a straw pile.

The big, old steam engine used to power the thresher was a wondrous machine. My earliest memories are of a steam engine —was it a Hart Parr?—so large it was deemed unsafe to cross the old wooden road bridge. My dad had to take down the fence so it could be moved across the pasture and cross the creek where the banks were shallow. It moved so slowly that it might take almost half a day to move it from one location to another and get it set up ready to work again.

There was a whistle on the old steam engine that was used to give signals, such as time to start, quitting time, etc. One of the greatest thrills was for some of the older boys to sneak out at night after all was quiet and use that last bit of steam to blow the whistle. The engine operator always seemed displeased about the prank, but surely it was all part of the game.

The fireman who had to fire up the engine and keep the steam pressure under control often would stay with the family where the machine was working, so he would be on hand before 5 a.m. to get things started. A timekeeper was appointed who kept track of the hours worked at each place. At the end of the season there was a threshers' meeting, when all the families involved got together. The hours were figured and payment was made accordingly. It was customary for the man who owned the threshing rig to furnish ice cream for all. What a delight that was! Remember, this was long before most farmers had electricity, so ice cream was a rare summer treat.

One could almost hear a collective sigh from the farmers and their families when this job was finished for another year. They knew that there would be a breather before the hard labor of corn picking began. It's hard to imagine the energy, muscle power and stamina necessary to accomplish this annual task.

Oat harvesting was hot, hard work for the men. But consider the women's work. There was no electricity, hence no refrigeration. There was no fresh meat unless a woman went to the butcher shop in town early in the morning or dressed about five or six chickens so they could be cooled in water from the deep well, which was cooler than water from the house well.

The large crews would have 20 to 24 men to feed, plus the women and children. Neighbor women and relatives would band together to prepare all this food as there were dinners, afternoon lunches and sometimes suppers to be served.

The cooks would vie with one another to serve the best and most tasty meals. Each lady had her specialty. She might be famous for her pies, one lady made a delicious white cake, another's meat loaf scored a hit. At our house pie was always served to the men on a set of beautiful hand-painted china pie plates. To my young mind, it always seemed strange to serve the men on these lovely delicate plates that were used only for "special company" otherwise. There were at least two kinds of pie to choose from; often a small piece of each was served.

With that many men to feed, there were always two tables of 12 to be waited on. Guess who got to do the running while the women were dishing up the food, then washing dishes for the next table? And before all the dishes were done, some of the cooks were preparing the lunch, which was taken out, so the men could eat in shifts and not stop the machine.

Since almost all bread was baked at home, along with the pies, cakes and cookies, the old cookstove was going from early morning until at least 8:30 each evening. Can you imagine how hot the house would get! Guess by the time we fell into bed at night, we were so tired we never noticed the temperature. Another job for the kids was hauling cobs and wood to be fed into the kitchen range. Oh, the delight of picking up corncobs in the hog yard!

And then there was the uncertainty; if it would rain suddenly and the men all went home, the cooks would have mountains of food prepared and no refrigeration to keep it. Or, after a rain the grain might be dry enough to start an hour before noon, hence a wild scramble to get dinner on the table.

Farming was not specialized in those days. Each farmer had hogs to feed, cows to milk and chickens to tend, so there were chores to do morning and night. Lots of farmers' wives and children got to do all the chores during the threshing season. There were gardens to tend also, as nearly all the food was grown at home. Then, too, many housewives had a rigid schedule for the housework: wash on Monday, iron on Tuesday, etc. It was always our fervent hope that the threshers wouldn't come on Monday, as the washing just had to go on.

Oh, the good old days—when men worked from sun to sun, but women's work was never done! For my part, I'll settle for electricity and all the modern conveniences we enjoy today!

Maxine A. Steele
Sutherland, Iowa

A Neighborhood Event

"Threshing" time in July and August was an annual opportunity for the entire neighborhood to work and visit together. One threshing machine was owned by an individual or as a neighborhood group. The men traveled from farm to farm threshing the oats or wheat until every farmer had been served.

Usually the younger children served as "water" boy or girl—riding their pony delivering stone jugs of water to quench the thirst of the hot and weary men in the field. The jugs were wrapped in wet burlap to keep the water cool.

The women gathered in the kitchen of the host farmer to prepare the noon meal, and on occasion the evening meal. Canned pork or beef, fried chicken, potatoes and gravy, cole slaw, green beans, corn or whatever vegetables were ready from the garden, along with homemade bread and pies and cakes were served—all cooked on a wood-burning cookstove.

With no refrigerators, it was a task to prepare food and keep it safe for eating. The milk and homemade butter containers were placed in burlap sacks and hung down into the well for cooling.

Pails of water and washpans were placed on benches on the lawn for the men and boys to wash in before coming inside to eat at the heavily laden dining tables. The women and girls always waited to eat until the men had returned to the field for work, then they could sit down to rest and eat as they began planning the next day's meal to serve the 10 to 20 men and boys. The final chore for that meal was shooing the flies out the door by using dishtowels—one in each hand. While one held the door open, two or three women or girls waved the dishtowels vigorously to rid the kitchen of the unwelcomed insects.

Threshing time was a time of hot, hard work, but it was also a time of camaraderie for the families, one that usually ended with a homemade ice cream social at the end of the season.

Margaret Blair
Lorimor, Iowa

Young Hired Men

Hired men were vital to the Nebraska wheat harvest during the 1940s and 1950s. To Dad, these young men were perpetual energy during a busy time. To Mom, they were bottomless stomachs to fill with home-grown food and homesick hearts that needed motherly words. To their three tow-headed children, most of the young men were the big brothers we didn't have in our family.

As the eldest, I recall Harvey, whose compassionate heart at the end of the day saw to it that the barefooted young ones didn't get in trouble about filthy feet. He would wash our feet in the horse tank and carry us to the house.

When Dad was hospitalized with a broken leg that required surgery, a neighbor boy helped Mom with the chores. He was inside once when Mom was cutting up a fryer. Our curious noses surrounded her as we stood on kitchen chairs observing the process. We shouted out the various body parts. (Mother had told us that the reproductive organs were tonsils. When she came to these parts she attempted to hide them, but our sharp eyes noticed them.) "There are the tonsils!" we chorused. The neighbor exited chuckling.

Another hired man was Calvin, whose sister was a long-time friend of Mother's. She lived about 30 miles away in town. Calvin was tall and had long legs; my short legs had trouble keeping up with him. One evening, as he was carrying two full pails of milk from the barn, I saw a chance to win a race with him! He was up to the challenge. Somehow he managed to beat me. How much milk was spilled, I don't recall.

Eddie was a freckled redhead from Washington's Vashon Island. This teenager's home had electricity and modern plumbing. Our Nebraska farm had kerosene lamps and a privy. Eddie brought a growing boy's appetite; we had few leftovers during the summer that Eddie worked for us. Eddie aided us kids in making a clubhouse, something we Nebraska youngsters knew little about. He helped us make simple chairs by removing three upper sides of wooden orange crates. Next he assisted us in lugging them up the barn's straight-up-and-down wooden ladder that led to the haymow, where the barn cats lived. We held our meetings in the haymow, with Eddie's assistance.

Louie was a minister's son who was studying to be a Lutheran minister. The young teal ducks on the pasture draw tempted him. When we returned from town one afternoon, we found a note on the kitchen table from Louie. It read: "There's a slightly picked 'chicken' in the wash house." Louie had taken one of Dad's rifles to the field and returned with a duckling. Mother couldn't prepare it for a meal, but we don't recall why it was unfit.

One summer during the 1950s I was attending summer school at a Nebraska college. Traveling home one weekend, I conversed with a fellow passenger on the Greyhound bus. He was a handsome Missouri college student who hoped to locate summer employment in Colorado. He was uncertain how he would get there because the bus that we were on went to Wyoming, not Colorado. I informed him that we lived near the Colorado border and that probably my folks could help him get there. (Secretly I was hoping that my dad would hire him!) Bob, the young man, worked that entire summer for Dad and nearby neighbors.

Dad occasionally hired older men but some of them weren't satisfactory workers. To us three, older men weren't a bit exciting, but we recall the young laborers with fond memories.

Joann Daubendiek
Ogallala, Nebraska

Tools of the Trade

The old farm shop was found on most farms. It was a building approximately 14 feet wide and 20 feet long. Usually it had two entrances, including a larger one to admit small equipment for repair, with a bench along one side sturdy enough for a heavy vise. There were shelves on the other side for bolts, repairs, etc.

Everything was arranged to a farmer's liking. In one end would be a hand-powered post drill and a foot-powered grindstone. There was a sliding window above the workbench and a chain from the ceiling with a hook to hang a lantern as there was no electricity in those old farm shops. Many farmers owned a large wooden chest where they kept their most prized tools. The shop usually contained a heavy anvil, as well as a few nail kegs for chairs, as neighbors often came to visit on rainy days. Scraps of wood, metal and leather were scattered around on the dirt floor.

Both of my grandfathers had one of these old farm shops. As a boy in the '20s, I well remember playing in the shop and sometimes whacking my fingers.

My wife of 57 years and I live on one of these farms. I was born in this house 78 years ago. I now keep my pickup in one of these old buildings.

Delbert Pilling
Wapello, Iowa

Life Without Modern Conveniences

There were nine in our family: five children, my parents and my mother's parents. There were also one or two hired men at times. When we were older, our friends' daughter came and stayed for a school year until she graduated from high school with my oldest sister. So there was always room for one or two more to eat or sleep, and we were brought up to share.

My earliest Christmas memory was when I got "Toodles," who had a composition head and a stuffed cloth body. My father would go with a horse-drawn sled or wagon on runners to the nearest larger town at Christmas, and a clerk named Mamie would select one item for each of us. I never remember my mother going, as my father always did all the shopping. The only time we went along was when we had to be fitted for shoes.

My three older siblings attended country school, and I remember what a treat it was to be allowed to visit. Later I met the teacher and she recalled my visits. By then a public school in town had been built so I started first grade there. We went in a horse-drawn bus-wagon with side curtains—it had wheels in good weather and runners in winter. My mother heated soapstones in the oven so our feet would stay warm. I must have been able to read when I started as I was 6 in March, and I was promoted to second grade after a few weeks. At home, I loved to play school.

In about 1920, we had a Dodge car with side curtains and running boards. We were moving to Wisconsin that fall, so in the summer, we set out— five children and our parents, to visit relatives in Minnesota. At one stage of the trip, we had a great deal of rain, and we ended up leaving the car and taking a train to Elbow Lake. Traveling with five children must have been quite an adventure.

In the fall of the year, it was a large event when the steam powered threshing rig came to thresh the shocks of grain from the field. The neighbors helped, and the men in our family helped when it was their turn. There were about a dozen extra men to feed for a couple of days. This meant a lot of food to cook and dishes to wash. We didn't have modern conveniences, so Mother put a wash bench outside with a pail of water, soap and towels and the men washed there before coming in to eat. I am not sure at what age I started washing dishes with my grandmother. We had two metal dishpans on the table; I washed and she wiped.

Now that I am in my 80s, I realize how much work my mother did. She was a seamstress before she was married and she had a domestic treadle machine on which she made all our clothes: dresses and coats, bloomers, etc. My grandmother pieced quilts by hand and made braided wool rugs for our bedrooms, which were very heavy to shake out of the windows every Saturday morning. She also crocheted doilies and knitted lace edgings for pillowcases. I am glad I had the experience of learning from my mother. It came in very handy after I had my two daughters.

Living on the farm probably taught me to appreciate more the conveniences we now have and to enjoy life to the fullest while we are young—I know I never missed what I didn't have!

Erma Hawkins
Tucson, Arizona

Dad Planted the Straightest Rows of All

When I was about 11 years old, I rode the binder pulled by an oil-pull tractor to cut wheat and oats. The old binder would cut the wheat with a sickle, then the wheat was pushed back on a canvas conveyer up to the binder, where it would tie a bundle with binding twine. Then it was kicked out onto a bundle carrier, and when I got five or six bundles in it, I would trip and release those bundles into even rows so they could be shocked and capped.

Dad would cut the timothy and clover hay for the horse barn and alfalfa hay for the cattle barn. After it was cut and cured by the sun, he would rake it in even rows and we could take the wagons to the field and fasten the hay loader on the back of the hay wagon. I would walk along the ground and drive the team until we had it loaded. Then I'd hitch the loader to the other wagon and do the same until that wagon was loaded too. Then we took both wagons to the barn where we had an old pair of white mules named Beck and Kate hitched to a rope and pulley that was fastened to the barn. A long rope was fastened to the big hay fork in front of the barn and I would drive these mules when Dad would holler, "Let's go." He'd have that big fork tromped into that hay on the wagon and it would pull about one-third of that load into the barn loft. I would pull a small rope to trip it and the hay would fall into the loft. My, that fresh hay always smelled so good.

Dad usually had all of the plowing done by the time school was out toward the last of April; then he would plant the field corn. Dad checked his corn then stretched a wire across the field. At the end of the field he would turn the horses back and get off the planter. He put the wire on and fastened it to the side of the planter, and he followed the marker across the field. The wire had notches on it that would trip the planter box, causing the corn to fall to the ground. The wheels were just so that they made the dirt cover the grains of corn as it passed over them. The neighbor said that Dad planted the straightest rows of all. When the corn came up it had to be cultivated about three times. Usually when the corn was laid by, as we called it, it was time to thresh the wheat and oats. I remember when

I was small, they would bring an old steam engine tractor pulling the separator to our farm. That was really fascinating to watch them thresh; when I got old enough I was the water boy. I would take our riding horse, put two water jugs across the saddle horn, and make the rounds of the field where they were loading the shocks on the wagon. Then I would take water to the threshing crew. I remember when they would thresh at our place, several neighbor men and women would come with their wagons. Men worked in the fields, and the women helped to get dinner ready. Those dinners of fried chicken, mashed potatoes, milk gravy and all the trimmings were a real treat.

Thurman Taylor
Carbondale, Illinois

Haying Time

Around 1943 haying was accomplished with a monkey tractor and a buck rake on our little farm in Collins, New York.

The so-called monkey tractor was a homemade affair consisting of a 1918 shortened-up Federal truck with a Studebaker engine.

To make the contraption work my Uncle Ham rigged up a wire stretcher with ropes and four pulleys that, when tightened, would lift the buck rake. The buck rake was made of mostly angle iron with pointed teeth on the ends and was attached to the front of the monkey tractor. It would gather the sweet smelling dry hay that had been deposited in huge piles by an old dump rake.

Hanging on for dear life, just for the thrill of hitting bumps in the hayfield, I would ride on the back of the monkey tractor.

The exhaust fumes would be so bad from riding there that I would get off occasionally to get a cold drink and some fresh air in my lungs.

My parents sold that first farm of my childhood a few years later, but I will never forget the sweet memories of haying time.

Teresa M. Fehlman
Gowanda, New York

Grain Stealing

When I was a child, it was not uncommon for some people to steal from their neighbors.

One particularly early morning, our granary door was open. As Dad went downstairs to take Mother a cup of tea because she was not feeling well, he thought the dog had opened the door. As she dozed, she thought she heard the granary door slam shut, so she assumed that Dad had closed it.

When he brought her tea to her bedside, he noticed that the door was closed and he was alarmed. He woke me and asked me to go with him. Sure enough one grain bin was completely empty. Someone had carried grain to a nearby road.

There was frost on the ground, so we followed the tracks to the roadside where a team and wagon had stood. Our neighbor's sack with his name on it was hung on the fence.

My dad contacted him and he said he had lost a couple sacks of timothy seed, so these were just a ruse.

Several weeks later, Dad was talking about the theft, when one man said that he saw a wagon partially full of grain sacks come into town at daylight. Of course grain cannot be identified, so it was a total loss. This man stole all the grain he could find to feed his horses.

Madonna L. Storla
Postville, Iowa

Threshing Rings

Threshing was an interesting time. Dad owned a threshing machine and threshed for six or seven neighbors as well as himself. Those in Dad's threshing ring helped each other. The day they threshed at our house, we girls sat in an old wagon seat beside the backyard gate and watched the wagons come. The rack wagons came first. Younger farmers handled the racks, drove to the field and loaded the wagons with bundles of oats. Grandpa was one of the older farmers, and drove one of the box wagons.

The bundles of oats were pitched into the feeder of the threshing machine. The box wagon had to be in position to catch the grain. Dad thought the man on the box wagon had the heavier duty because he had to scoop the oats into the empty bin in the granary. After the grain bin was filled, oats were hauled to the elevator in White Heath to be sold.

Corn harvest started around October 20th. I remember hearing horses trotting down the lane at daylight, the empty wagon rattling, and Dad whistling a merry tune as he drove to the field. We noticed farmers shucking corn in fields all around as we walked to school. We heard ears of corn, clean of shucks, make a "bang" when the farmers tossed corn into the wagon and the ears hit the bump board. The bump board prevented the corn from going over the wagon. When the wagon was full, the men drove to the crib to dump; farm scales were used to weigh the load. Wagons were pulled into place beside the corn crib, and chains were fastened to the front wheel axles in order to lift the wagon high enough to force the corn to roll out. A motor moved the elevator chains that carried corn up and into the top of the crib. After dinner, the men went back to the field. The hired man was anxious to shuck 100 bushels a day. Dad paid 5 cents per bushel.

Farmers were tired each evening after a day of shucking corn. Their gloves would get wet on frosty mornings, and their hands would get chapped and sore. Their backs would ache from reaching to the ground to get corn from broken stalks.

We girls had more chores to do in autumn. All three lamps had to be filled with kerosene. Lamp flues had to be washed. More coal and corncobs had to be carried to the house to be used in the heating stove and the cookstove.

Mother enjoyed autumn. The long busy summer days were over, and the cellar was stocked with the fruits of her labor: canned food, late cabbage, turnips, onions, apples, pears, potatoes and pumpkins.

Spring was a glorious season for us children. We picked purple violets from along the roadside on our walk home from school and knelt in the lily bed in the front yard to breathe the fragrance of hyacinths blooming there. We climbed to the haymow and caught baby pigeons to pet. We caught the baby calves and tried to tame them. We pulled fish worms from the ground and fed the worms to the baby chickens. It was funny to watch two little chickens, one at each end of the fish worm, pulling on the worm, like tug-of-war.

One morning in May, after the corn was planted, Dad noticed a long circus train on the railroad tracks north of the farm. He came to the house and said, "If I can get the automobile started, we are all going to the circus in Champaign." He worked on the car all morning and got it running good, and we went to the circus. It was about 25 miles from home. The trapeze performers were beautiful and daring; the clowns were funny. I didn't like to see the wild animals loose in a ring and doing tricks. I thought I'd rather see lions, tigers and elephants in our picture books at home. Dad bought each of us a box of Cracker Jacks.

Special entertainment was not a priority in those days. There was peace and harmony in our home, and a restful night at the close of a busy day.

Mrs. Guyneth Walker
Atwood, Illinois

Grandpa's Lemon Tree

I grew up on the south side of Chicago. When I was a little girl, we still had a neighbor who walked her cow down the road past our house to take it to a pasture on the edge of town. The lady next door kept chickens. We had a fairly large backyard. My grandfather loved phlox. He had clumps of every different kind. People came from all over to see them. Grandpa also had a lemon tree— perhaps the only one in Chicago. It was in a huge tub. Every spring he dug a hole in the center of our pocket-sized front lawn and buried the pot. In the fall, he dug it up again. All my uncles had to help. Winters the lemon tree was kept in front of a window in the basement. It smelled lovely. The lemons were the giant kind. We never had any. Grandpa gave them to people like his boss, the preacher and very good friends.

World War II came along when I was in eighth grade. Victory garden plots were plowed up and loaned to anyone who would tend them. Ours was on 115th and Halsted Street, still a rural area then. My father went into the Navy. Grandpa got our garden going. The car was put up on blocks—no tires or gasoline—so we had to walk back and forth. Most evenings found us watering or pulling weeds until dark. Grandma and Mom canned everything they could. I still keep a garden today, because I love fresh tomatoes and corn.

As a teen, I loved tomatoes too. I would line up five or six on the windowsill and lay in the hammock with a book, reading and eating tomatoes. One year my folks sent me to a tomato farm. I helped with the harvest. Most of the young men were off at war so I was needed. They painted my fingernails with a red color. That was the color of the tomatoes to be picked. I could pick the very ripe ones, but they were for me to eat, not for sale. The lighter and green tomatoes were left for future harvesting.

Other summers I was sent to an uncle's farm in Michigan. We picked currants and black raspberries. I preferred the currants because there were bees in the raspberries. I didn't make much—just enough for my room and board and for roller skating in town on Saturday night. My uncle spoke German, so he was given some German prisoners of war to help with the harvest. They were nice lads and seemed happy to be out of the war.

Mom always wanted me to marry one of the boys from a neighboring town. Their folks were in our church and were wealthy onion farmers. I said I wanted to marry a professional man, so I saved my money and went to the university. There I met my husband, who was studying to be an electronics engineer. We are retired now and we have a pecan orchard in Arizona. I guess it was destiny; I married a farmer after all.

Eleanor Lindemulder Mattausch
Benson, Arizona

Baling Hay in the 1940s

I have been thinking of the old-time methods used in farming. Having been a farmer's wife for six decades, I have seen several changes, but what especially comes to mind is our hay baling in the early 1940s.

We were still using horses some, along with a John Deere tractor. We had a stationary baler that was attached to the tractor with a long wide belt.

First the tractor was used for mowing the hay. Then the hay was raked with horses. When we started the actual baling—I say "we" because I had a part in it too—a team of horses was hooked to a bull rake, one at each side. The bull rake had several wooden teeth that ran under the hay, and was then brought up beside the baler.

The baler took at least four or five people to operate: one to pitch the hay in, one to "block" and stick the wire through from one side, one to tie the wire on the other side, one to move the bales out of the way and one to run the bull rake. Of course one of these people had to keep an eye on the tractor too, as it was idling several yards away from the work and sometimes would overheat.

The system required pitching the hay into the rack, where a large fork affair would plunge the hay down. More hay was put in. When the bale became a certain size, it was my job to shout "block" and everything stopped. I would put a homemade wooden square block, the size of the small part of the bale, in to divide the bales. I then stuck two baling wires through, and the fellow on the other side tied the wires securely, then the whole process would start again. We only had three or four of the blocks, so I had to retrieve each for use later. Sometimes the plunger would come down on the block and smash it to pieces. It took very delicate timing to know exactly when to halt the process. It allowed no time for daydreaming.

It was very dangerous for the fellow pitching the hay in, as the fork with big teeth respected neither people nor things. We were lucky and avoided any catastrophes.

This job took place in the hottest part of summer. It was a hot, dirty job but I enjoyed having such an important responsibility. The men all bragged on me because I did the job competently.

Della Whitesell
El Dorado Springs, Missouri

Loved Life as a Dairy Hand

Can you imagine a 15-year-old boy from the big city working as a farm hand on a dairy farm in the great state of Vermont? Well, that was me 51 years ago.

I had some cousins living in Saint Albans and wanted to be near the family one summer. Since my mother, aunt, uncle, brother and cousin went to the Catskills for the summer, I was bored. Well, I took the train from Grand Central to St. Albans, met my other family and after a few days went to the farm bureau to get a job on a farm.

I arrived on the farm in early June and got right on the job. The next morning I was awakened at 4:30 a.m. by the boss, had a cup of coffee and went to the night pasture with the dogs to get the cows into the barn. While one dog went into the pasture, the other dog stayed with me to assure that the cows would head toward the barn and not the other way.

During the month I was there, I was taught to use a milking machine, to strip cows, to put the tack on the pair of enormous horses we had, hook them to the wagon and drive them by myself, to slop the hogs and feed all the other animals we had. I worked from 4:30 a.m. to about 5:00 p.m. when the herd was returned to the night pasture. I became a pro at this work before I left for a job in the carnival business. I can say that I ate well, and even though this was really hard work, I loved every minute of it. It was quite an experience for me.

Joseph H. Cohen
Rego Park, New York

Treasuring Our Years on the Farm

"How dear to my heart are the scenes of my childhood. When fond recollections present them to view." I remember awakening on cold winter mornings and hearing my dad shoveling coal into the furnace. As I descended the stairs, the aroma of bacon would rise to meet me. Every morning my mother would prepare a breakfast of bacon, eggs, fried potatoes, homemade bread, oatmeal and coffee.

Life on the farm at that time would probably be boring for today's generation. We had no electricity nor indoor plumbing, which meant no electric lights and no household appliances for the kitchen or for cleaning the house, but we managed very well. I remember and still marvel at the amount of work my mother managed to do in a day. With nine of us in the family, she would bake 10 loaves of bread every other day. She raised 100 or more chickens every year, getting up at least once during the night to make sure the chicks didn't huddle together and smother each other. She managed to make several quilts during her lifetime and prepared three big meals each day. When I was quite small I would watch her scrubbing clothes on a washboard and rinsing them out in a tub of water, twisting them to get the water out and then taking them outdoors to hang on the clothesline. She ironed clothes with heavy old irons with interchangeable handles like those found in antique shops or museums today. She canned vegetables and fruit and lined the shelves in the basement with enough food to last a year. Although we were poor and we had to wear hand-me-down clothes, we had plenty to eat.

The most exciting day on the farm was butchering day, when neighbors came to help butcher five or six hogs. I would rise early in the morning and help my dad fill a large black kettle with water. I would put logs and corncobs under the kettle, and my dad would pour kerosene on the cobs and throw a match on them. Within an hour the water would be very hot. After the hogs were killed they were put in the scalding water and the hairs could be easily scraped from them. I wanted to skip school on butchering day but my mother would never allow it. When the school day was over I would run all the way home and eat cracklings till I was full. Although most of the butchering was over by the time I came home the hams still had to be wrapped. We would pour salt over the hams, wrap them in newspapers, then wrap a gunnysack around them and hang them in a shed, where in the summertime the temperature would be above 100 degrees.

We studied our lessons by the light of a kerosene lamp and did many chores by lantern light. Baths were taken by carrying buckets of water from an outside well to the basement and pouring the water into a galvanized washtub. Needless to say bath days were few and far between in the winter, as it was very cold in our basement.

We had an old radio that ran off of a car battery and was our source of entertainment as well as a connection with the outside world. My brother and I never missed "Gangbusters," which was our favorite program. After much use the battery began to fade out, and each day we had to move closer and closer to the radio. Finally it gave out completely and that was the end, as we could not afford a new battery. The other connection with the outside world was the large wooden telephone that hung on the dining room wall. Each household had its own ring. Ours was a long and a short, but every time it rang we could hear one receiver after another being lifted to listen in on the conversation. Of course if it rang for a neighbor we too would listen in. It was a common practice.

An old tree stood at the side of the road a quarter of a mile from home. Many times my brother and I would walk to the tree, lay down in the grass, and permit our imagination to take us as far as we dared to let it. To this day when I visit the old house, where my sister still lives, I look at the old tree, which is still standing, and let childhood memories return.

On January 7, 1940, rural electrification was introduced to our community. I marveled as I went from room to room turning on lights. The next morning I departed to serve in the United States Navy. Two years later as I stood on the deck of the battleship *Tennessee* on December 7, 1941, at Pearl Harbor, the Japanese attacked and destroyed most of the United States Pacific fleet. Within minutes after the attack began I fell wounded from shrapnel. On that morning America lost its innocence. Boys instantly became men and the world changed forever, but we who were lucky enough to be reared in a rural community—even during the Great Depression—will always treasure and remember those wonderful years of our childhood on the farm.

Jack Doyle
Taylorville, Illinois

The Ford Tractor

We had a Ford tractor on a 160-acre farm during the war years of the 1940s. My brother was 14 when somehow he fell off and the tractor ran over him. Dad could not get men to work on the farm as they were all at war. He had to work off the farm to make a living, so I had to help out, even though I was a 13-year-old girl. I drove for hay baling, I plowed people's gardens and I pulled big trucks out of the mud up on the unpaved highway a quarter-mile from our house. I helped pay my way through college by driving that Ford. I pretty well knew most of its nuts and bolts.

One day I was plowing away, and at the end of the row, as I lifted the plow, my tractor tipped over. The axle had snapped off and the big rear wheel fell under the tractor, keeping it from tipping clear over.

When we had wheat to shock, Dad would get several boys from town to come help. They didn't know how to shock and theirs would fall over. They also did not know how to get the water out of the carburetor. I kept busy all day keeping the tractor going and fixing their shocks.

I also kinda felt I got the worst end of the deal when the threshers all came. I had to do the girl stuff, like clean the chickens and peel the potatoes for the lunch, plus wash the dishes! I had to drive the tractor to pull the wagons for the shocks of wheat or haul the grain to the barn. But then everyone had to do all they could to get the harvest done.

Some of the neighbors wondered then if I'd ever give up my

jeans and wear a dress. I married a preacher and had four children, so I've worn lots of dresses after all!

Gloria Williams
Grandview, Missouri

Good Old Days

Older people talk about the good old days. We did have some good times, even though we went through the Depression.

My mother cooked on a range that burned wood. It was our duty to keep the wood box beside the stove filled.

There was a reservoir on the side of the range for water. The range kept the water hot and we could use it to wash dishes in the dishpan on a table. No sink, no dishwasher, no electricity. My mother ironed with flat irons. We kept them on the back of the stove to stay hot. When we went to iron, we fastened a handle on the iron. In the winter, when it was cold and we slept upstairs with no heat, we would wrap the iron in heavy towels and take them to bed with us to keep our feet warm. Sometimes we would fill a hot-water bottle and use it to keep warm.

The rest of the house was heated by a potbellied stove. Some burned wood and some coal. My father would bank the fire in the heater with wood to last through the night. In the morning there would be enough coals left to restart the fire. The room would soon be warm.

The kitchen range had to be started each morning. You can imagine how hot the range would be to cook on in the hot summertime. Later on Mother had a kerosene stove to use in the summer.

We had no refrigerator or piped-in water. If you were lucky, you might have a pitcher pump inside to pump in water from the well or from the cistern that caught rain water. It would make your hair soft when you washed your hair in the rain water. Otherwise you would carry buckets of water into the house from the well.

At night we used kerosene lamps to read or sew by. We cleaned the chimney each day and kept the lamps filled.

My mother had to bake bread several times a week. She would make some of the dough into cinnamon rolls. We also churned our own butter. Sometimes that was my job.

We had a big garden and canned all our fruits and vegetables for winter use. Mom would can beef, sausage and cure and smoke our own ham and bacon in the winter. It was not unusual for people to can 1000 quarts of food. We might not have had a lot of money, but we had plenty to eat.

Mildred Swinford
Keokuk, Iowa

Dad Appreciated Help in the Field

Grandpa had four daughters and may have wished for a son at wheat harvest time. That was when horses and wagons were used and the work was hard. When my mother was 16, she volunteered to help her dad in the field. He agreed to give her a try, and she proved to be very helpful. Her proudest moment came when he trusted her to drive a wagonload of wheat to town. It was an awesome responsibility to handle the team of horses the six miles to town, but the hardest part came at the grain elevator. The wagon had to be positioned in just the right place for the wheat to dump in the bin.

She accomplished the task and carefully drove the team and empty wagon back home and handed her dad the receipt for the wheat. He was very pleased. She didn't know just how pleased until a couple of weeks later when her sisters told her that their dad had something for her. Curious, she went to him and asked if he had something he wanted to give her. Not being accustomed to giving gifts, he hesitantly handed her a beautiful gold bracelet that he had bought in the jewelry store. Although he didn't say it, she understood that it was to show his appreciation for her help in the field. She kept the gold bracelet all her life.

Penny M. Smith
Oberlin, Kansas

Harvesting in Years Gone By

The methods of harvesting grain have changed completely since I became a farmer's wife in the late 1930s. Nearly all the farmers raised a patch of oats and a patch of wheat. In June, usually, the crops were ready to cut with a grain binder, a piece of machinery that was pulled by a team of horses. Besides cutting the grain, it tied it into bundles. Then the older boys or a hired man would stack the bundles—each the same size—in shocks in the field.

The bundles were stood on end, with the grain at the top, and then a bundle or two laid flat across the top. This was to protect the grain from the weather, as it had to stay in this position for a month or more until it was ready to thresh.

Then came Threshing Day. The owner of the threshing machine went to each farm. The different farmers went along too, trading work, as it took several people to do all of this. The owner could usually tell how long he would be at a certain farm, which allowed him to tell the next farmer when to be ready. The weather was a factor too, because everything stopped in case of rain.

Several men with horses and hay wagons came and hauled big loads of the cured bundles of grain into the threshing machine, where they would pitch it into the machine with pitchforks. Another wagon would be waiting to unload just as soon as one was empty. On the other side the straw came out a spout and made a huge straw stack, which the farmer used for many purposes: livestock bedding, mulch for gardening, feed, and sometimes, often in fact during the Depression, the oat straw was used in straw ticks for the beds. Some people had feather ticks but few had mattresses.

Usually the threshing could be finished in a day or a day and a half, depending on the size of the crop. Then they went on to the next farm. The farm boys usually were available to keep a supply of drinking water to all the men. This threshing work was very hard and hot work.

Della Whitesell
El Dorado Springs, Missouri

I Can Always Go Home

On October 18, 1948, my mom and dad were married in a small Catholic country church in Doniphan, Kansas. They were both raised on farms by German-Irish parents and were used to working very hard. They had mules and horses instead of tractors back then. My folks raised five of us—I have an older sister and three younger brothers. Being older than our brothers, my sister and I became farmhands early. We started raking hay and cultivating corn when we were 10 years old. My dad raised corn, wheat, beans and hay as well as cattle and pigs. We grew up on a farm that started out with one milk cow and a pony for each of us kids. Now they have a dairy farm milking up to 100 cows twice a day and two pairs of mules that they use to feed the cattle and do a lot of their farm work with, such as plowing, cultivating and shucking corn. When you pull into the driveway you'll see dozens of cats and kittens and one beautiful black-and-white dog that wants to get in your path.

I used to love going to the fields and watching my dad as he combined wheat. We would stand up on the side of the big truck and watch as the wheat came shooting out of the combine. We would get covered in dust and start sneezing but it didn't matter. We were having fun! Mom would bring a lunch out to the field so that Dad wouldn't have to stop combining. We would have the best bologna sandwiches I thought I would ever taste. It seemed like such a treat to be eating outside in a hot Kansas wheatfield. Now I take my nephews and nieces in the pickup truck to watch my dad or one of my brothers as they combine wheat. They enjoy watching the wheat harvest just as much as I did when I was their age.

We started out driving small tractors such as C's and H's. One day my sister and I were supposed to go cultivate this cornfield that was just a bit muddy yet. Dad told us to be very careful not to get stuck. Karen and I decided that if one of us got stuck we would just stay put, and when the other one came over the hill she would help get the stuckee out. Well, wouldn't you know it, I got stuck. I waited for what seemed to be an eternity for my sister to come up over that hill so she could pull me out. I waited and waited, but no tractor came. I finally jumped down off the tractor and started the long walk up the hill. I couldn't believe my eyes when I saw my sister and her tractor stuck in the mud also. We both kind of laughed and walked to the house together to get another tractor to pull us both out. My brothers eventually took over for us as they grew older and I breathed a sigh of relief not to have to get on those tractors much anymore.

In the summer we would all go to the local church picnics. We had the best times at those picnics. First we would eat a wonderful dinner cooked by the ladies of the church, then Dad would give each of us our own money to go play bingo, or toss the ring over the bottle to win a small prize.

One thing that we used to do as a family was ride our horses to move the cattle from one pasture to another. We would saddle up and start the long trip down the hills early in the morning. One time we stopped to roast hot dogs and marshmallows over an open fire. By the time we got back to the house and got off of our horses we were walking very bow-legged. I can remember laughing at everyone as they dismounted until it came my turn to get down and I could barely walk.

My sister and my brothers all live on farms with their families now. My two sons and I are the only "city slickers" in the bunch. My sons have pretty much grown up on my folks' farm as well. They have put up numerous bales of hay and fixed a few fences. When they were little we used to put them to work shelling peas or breaking beans for my mom to can. They too learned to ride horses, which they both love to do. My dad and younger brother have run a dairy farm for more than 15 years. My sons have helped milk cows and clean up the milk barn many times. Although they have come to the conclusion that milking and farming is not for them, they do enjoy going out to the farm and helping out.

When I go to visit my folks and walk in the front door, I never know if I might run into a newborn calf needing my mom's special care, or maybe a boxful of beautiful yellow ducklings that my dad just brought home for the grandkids to play with and watch grow.

But one thing I do know for sure is that I was raised with a lot of love on that farm and that it is a place that I can always go home to.

Louise A. Hill

Atchison, Kansas

Topping Onions

Back in 1923 we lived on a farm near Pleasant Valley, Iowa. Many farmers around there would put in an onion crop at that time and ask the area children to come top onions for 7 cents a bushel. I was 10 years old then. My mother took the five of us children to a neighbor's onion field and we all topped onions. At the end of the day I was paid a silver dollar, a half dollar and a quarter for 25 bushels topped. I was so thrilled. Of course we had to put half of it in our savings account. But we all kept topping onions for years. Most of us managed to top 100 bushels a day! Dad used his truck to haul the onions to the train depot. That kept the whole family busy for a couple of weeks each summer. It also taught us to save part of our money. We still had those bank accounts in 1932, when, on December 22nd of that year, our bank closed! We did get all our money gradually, and we kept on adding to our bank accounts.

In 1930 my sister and I graduated from Davenport High School. After that we taught in one-room schools. When the banks closed in 1932, I hadn't cashed my paycheck that month as I had signed up for life insurance. That made me the only one in the family who had some cash, my monthly paycheck of $95. The insurance agent didn't get his money for a couple of months after that, as we used what money we had to buy necessary groceries.

In later years, there were no longer any young people who were willing to top onions for such a small amount of money, so gradually the onion farmers all gave up! I am glad there was an opportunity like that for us. I am sure it taught us to save part of our money, and today we are much better off because of that.

Olivia M. Wiese

Davenport, Iowa

Family Closeness Lasts a Lifetime

We bought our farm when I was 11. It seemed we spent a good part of the summer hauling wheat to market. My job was leveling it out, either in the combine bin or the truck. Mom and I made countless trips to the elevator, then one day the trailer hitch broke and dumped the wheat, not in any regular dry ditch, but in the only water-filled lagoon we passed through on our eight-mile trip to town. When we "righted" the trailer, we spent some frantic times trying to rescue the water-soaked wheat. The waterfowl that inhabited the place were very happy for our mistake.

On Tuesday nights, there were the outdoor shows. Everyone would gather, buy groceries and visit. We sat on low wooden benches, swatted the mosquitoes and followed the adventures of our mostly western movie heroes.

Help was hard to find, so Mom worked in the field alone with Dad. I was the chief cook and watcher of my little sister. This began our closeness that continues though we are separated by 1400 miles.

One of the duties I had was to provide meals. We had a hired hand one year who liked catsup on everything. I watched him put it on eggs in the morning, and then continue all day until one day he took one of my chocolate drop cookies with a walnut on top, put it on his plate and added catsup. After one bite he sputtered and choked. "I thought those were hamburgers," he finally coughed out. He'd finally found something that wasn't made better with catsup. He also put a hole in the ceiling of his bedroom one day when he was cleaning out his gun because he forgot to take out the bullets. We were grateful that the hole wasn't in him.

Mom and I always cleaned the grain bins. One time we discovered a mouse nest. Mom got out quickly, and I had the job of killing them all. She also didn't go into the cave because she didn't like the lizards. I grew to respect them for they had their own special beauty.

We pumped water from the well, and I learned to take a bath in a little water with a washcloth. One night I got caught in the spare room taking a sponge bath when neighbors dropped in to visit in the parlor. It was a long time before my mother realized where I was and rescued me. I was not about to walk out with a towel wrapped around me.

Reading was my main hobby but by a kerosene lamp it was hard to see, so evenings were limited to listening to a battery operated radio, sleeping and talking. When rural electricity came through, it was the miracle we had all hoped for.

My sister's farm life is much different now.

Barbara J. Epley-Shuck
Whitesboro, New York

Dad's Sorghum Molasses

My dad realized early in his life that farming a few acres was not going to bring in enough cash to raise a big family. A child was born every two and a half to three years from 1907 to 1932, until there were nine of us. One of his schemes to provide for us was making molasses every fall. This occupation requires a certain amount of skill as well as hard labor. The skill and equipment he obtained from my grandfather, but he experimented and failed many times before he became an expert at making the finest molasses in the county.

The first step was planting the sugar cane and tending it all summer, hoping for a good crop. How well I remember being taken to the sugar cane field to strip the cane. Slashing the green leaves away from the cane stalks was no fun, as the leaves were sharp and thick. After this was accomplished, the cane was cut low to the ground and hauled to the mill for grinding out the juice.

The mill was a series of cogs, where someone had to feed in the stalks a few at a time. A single horse was led round and round to make the cogs turn. This was often a child's job. As the juice was extracted, it was strained into a barrel.

The pan for boiling was set over a deep pit where a suitable fire was made and kept going as long as it took to boil off a batch of molasses. The juice was transferred to the pan and a careful watch began. Skimming off the foam and stoking the fire was a constant three- to four-hour vigil. When it was just right, and only Dad knew this, it was poured into one-half or one-gallon jars or buckets for sale or our own use. Those who brought their own cane also brought their own containers.

How pleasant it is to remember the pungent odor of that juice boiling on a clear frosty morning. Dad's goal was to boil off two batches a day, which meant the children had to do chores before going to school. Mama also had to help on top of all her numerous family duties.

One of the rewards of this process was the customers who came for miles around to get their molasses supply. My parents enjoyed these visits with friends whom they perhaps did not see but once a year.

I'm sure Dad was glad when the last batch was made, the pan cleaned and stored for another year, but I'm also sure he felt good knowing a job was well done and he was providing for his family.

Auda B. Bratcher
Raytown, Missouri

Butchering Time

When I was a teenager in the '40s, living on a farm, neighbors were very far apart. Our closest neighbors were about three-quarters of a mile away as the crow flies. They and my parents helped each other in any way they could, such as working with horses or working in the fields together.

The event that stands out clearly in my mind was butchering time. It was so cold out, and heating the water to scald an animal was a chore in itself. Cutting up the meat with no electricity was a hard, messy job. We canned what we could, then ground the lard down and rendered it, which meant melting it down. It was dangerous working with the hot grease. Eating the fresh meat came next—that was the good part. Frying fresh liver to eat with some home-baked bread and butter—with a little slice of onion if you wanted—nothing ever tasted so good.

Many times we walked across the fields to our neighbors' house for homemade ice cream, and sometimes they came to our house. A flashlight was our only light to get back home; there were no space lights around to guide you. If the moon was shining it was a big help. I was always worried about stepping on a snake, but I never did.

Lucille Wohler
Clay Center, Kansas

The Milk Separator

We moved into town when I was 5. One of the things I remember was the old Jersey cow. She was huge. Dad would come home from work and milk her before he ate supper. Lots of times I would go with him to the barn. We had a cold water milk separator that he would pour the milk into. The way I remember, it was blue, round, tall and to me, big. Dad would pour two or three buckets of milk into it when he milked the Jersey. He would also give some to the many cats that always knew when it was milking time.

Mom would go out the next morning and drain the milk from a spout near the bottom. Milk would drain out first, then half-and-half, then the real cream. I remember the milk separator well, because one day I decided to help Mom by draining about a gallon of milk into a dirty bucket. I got a major lecture, but the cats enjoyed the extra milk that day.

My brothers and sisters don't recall the milk separator the way I do. Thirty some years later when I saw it in storage it brought back some memories of the farm. Strangely, the separator was not as huge as I remembered it. But everything does look bigger in a 5-year-old's eyes, and those memories do not change with age.

Janice Gatlin
Osawatomie, Kansas

The Wood Splitter

"Awake!"
The wren sings,
"The sun is shining!
No rain! No rain today!"

Hurry! Dress. Help! Where's my dentures?
The search is on. Thirty-one minutes wasted. Found!
But where's my shoe? Lost again? Maybe it's downstairs?
That darling puppy? Maybe it's by the back door under the tree?
Breakfast: Cereal, eggs, bacon, toast, fruit juice, coffee? Why bother?

The sun is shining! The wood needs splitting! Get the key! Start
the tractor!
Attach the splitter! Drive to the woodpile. Roll or lift a tough
block on the platform.
Push the forward lever. Presto! That oak knot is ready for winter!

Repeat the maneuver over and over.
Thank God somebody
invented
this
Wood Splitter!
Lucille Stanek Jenkins
Jackson, Michigan

No Time to Sit Under the Shade Tree

My ex-husband and I bought a farm in 1940 and began farming
two years after we were married. We milked cows, separated milk
and sold cream. From our cream checks we bought our groceries,
gas for the car, kerosene for the lamps and anything our son, and
later our daughter, needed.

I raised, canned and later froze the food from my garden for our
family of four, the hired men and other men it took to get the farm

work done. I baked our bread, dried corn for winter use, made 14-day pickles and cold-packed beef. I kept my cookies in a stone jar in the cellar; they stayed fresh when kept cool. I raised 300 chickens every year, from which I froze fryers and old hens. From my egg money I bought groceries and hot lunches for my children at Tipton Consolidated School, the first consolidated school west of the Mississippi River. My hard farm work and chores helped to feed 65 other people every day, which every farmer did at that time.

I made my own laundry soap, because there were no laundry or dish detergents then. I boiled my white clothing in a wash boiler. The house was the only one built on the land after it was homesteaded and was not modern in any way until I gave up half the bedroom for a bathroom in about 1954. Then I also had water in the kitchen and modern cupboards. We got electricity when the REA provided it. It was such a blessing, because it allowed us to have a refrigerator, electric lights and later, a freezer. Cooking for so much farm help was simplified with modernization and food freezing.

The house we lived in was old and small, but I kept it shining like a mansion. I always used enamel paint on the floors, woodwork and walls. I painted the linoleum when it was worn and stippled it with bright paint and a sponge. I dug violets from the creek pasture and timber by the bucketfuls and planted a border of them completely around the house. I had climbing roses and a row of bridal wreath along one side of the lawn to make our backyard private. I planted a weeping willow in the orchard and enjoyed it there because it shed no twigs to bother in mowing the lawn. We had a big shade tree in the back 40, but I was always helping to make hay, sow oats or husk corn, so I never did get to sit under that shade tree.

We lived nearly 10 miles from town, and it took the children an hour to get to the schoolhouse on the bus. Farming was not just a way to make a living; it was a way of life.

Elaine L. Nebergall
Tipton, Iowa

The Butter Churn

Reprinted with permission. Women's Household, *January 1987, House of White Birches, 306 East Parr Road, Berne, IN 46711.*

Do you remember when folks who lived in the country had at least one family cow and the milk from it provided enough butter-fat to be churned into butter? We always had a couple of good milk cows on our farm, so the chore of churning butter was always there and was especially relegated to us kids. Some cows' milk made white butter, while others' made yellow butter. I think it may have been the milk from the Guernsey cows that made yellow butter. After the cream was skimmed from the milk, Mother would place it on the hearth near the fire, until it "turned" or soured. This took a couple of days at least. As I recall, most of the churns were two-and-a-half- to three-gallon size, although some may have been larger.

By the time it became my job, we were using the stone crock-type churn, with a picture of an Indian on the side near the top. Dashers were homemade from a broomstick, with wooden pieces nailed to the end. When it was my turn to churn, I always played a game of counting. I tried hard to count to 1000 without stopping if I could. That seemed to make the butter come faster. Sometimes I would just chant the words, "Come, butter, come." I was always very sure that this made the butter come faster. (As a rule it took only about a half hour or so, but to a child a half hour seemed like such a long time.) At times, when the butter was slow in coming, Mom would add just a bit of warm water to the milk. She never liked to do this, however, as she said the butter was not as good.

After the churning was finished, Mom took the butter flakes from the milk and formed them into neat little pats or cakes. Some folks had a spring house where they kept their milk and butter. We had a cistern. Later we got a kerosene refrigerator, which kept the products much better. Do you remember these refrigerators? Ours was a Cold Spot from Sears, Roebuck and Company. The wick and burner were hard to keep going, but it worked pretty well, and we enjoyed the luxury of having such an appliance.

After the Tennessee Valley Authority completed its project, we got electric power wired into our house. Mom got an electric churn, and things were never the same again. That was in late 1949 or early 1950. We kept the old churn as a standby, and from time to time I had the chore of churning by hand. I still live on the farm, but we haven't milked a cow in years. These days we buy our milk and butter from the supermarket, but to me, nothing will ever replace the wonderful taste of home-churned butter and hot corn bread.

Lawrence M. Mallicoat

Whitesburg, Tennessee

We Worked and Played Together

My husband started working on the farm when he was 10 years old. By the time he graduated from eighth grade he began working full time for $10 a month room and board. It was hard work and not many breaks were given. One place he worked he had to walk several miles to town on Saturday night to see his mother. The food was not always plentiful and Sunday night supper was mostly bread and milk. This was not much of a diet for a still-growing boy. After about a year another farmer offered a job that paid $30 a month, room and board, better victuals and a horse to ride to town. This was heaven for a young man.

Better and better jobs came along as the young man grew to manhood. Finally he moved north to bigger and better farms and met his future wife. After we married we moved to a farm where we lived primitively by today's standards. Much of this was difficult for me but I survived. The biggest fly in my ointment was the old wood cookstove in the kitchen. I had never cooked on such a monster and didn't even know how to start a fire. Lucky for me, my husband did. The reservoir, filled with hot water, was wonderful to me as we didn't have a hot-water heater. Pumping the pitcher pump in the kitchen to get cistern water was a great convenience. This water was only for dishwashing, cleaning and bathing. The well was out by the barn and had a hand pump.

Once I mastered the cookstove, I loved it. There is nothing to compare with a pot of soup cooked slowly all day or oatmeal set to cook on the back of the banked down stove overnight. Chicken and dumplings melt in your mouth when slow simmered on a cast iron giant. This same stove heated the copper wash boiler for doing the laundry and our bath water too. Clothes washing was an all-day undertaking at that time. My husband filled the wash boiler for me before he went to milk the cows. The water was good and hot by the time he came in for breakfast. He filled my washtub and rinse tub. Then I began the job of rubbing the clothes on the board. The linens and underwear were easy but those denim pants were very hard. I usually had to soak them the night before. Rubbing on the washboard is not exactly a beauty treatment for the knuckles. But I did it until one day my widowed father chanced to arrive as I was doing my wash and saw me hunched over the board. Since he possessed an almost-new Maytag wringer washer, which he seldom used, he soon saw to it that my days of washboard slavery were over. Washday became a comparative breeze for me. We still had to heat and carry water but my knuckles healed up and my back uncrooked. While the Maytag did the work, I could do other things.

The farm is a place where the work is never done. You just put in 15 or 16 hours and collapse. It is not like that so much now, but back then it was. I had a big garden to tend, barn work to do, and in time, four children to raise. Those were busy years. We didn't have central heating, only the old wood-heating stove. The cookstove provided heat for the kitchen. You just wore a lot of clothes.

Wintertime on the farm meant the chores were twice as hard and food became the focus of the day. My mainstays were soups, stews, chili, meat loaf, Swiss steak and chicken and dumplings. Desserts were bread pudding, cobblers, cakes and doughnuts. I also made a lot of coffee cake, which was Dad's favorite. I let my girls experiment to their hearts' content; whatever didn't turn out went over the back fence where some critter found a treat. We weren't wasteful but accidents when learning to cook do happen. Seeing that my girls could put out a good meal was more important to me. My biggest delight was the first time I had a birthday cake that I didn't have to bake myself.

Least you think we never had any fun, I am here to say we did. We had a pony named Beauty for the children. They loved her. We had dogs, cats, rabbits, birds and even a goat as pets. Our greatest enjoyment was going camping at Berry Land, a nearby campground. There we could fish, swim, picnic and just enjoy life. For a dollar a car we had it all. We also took a vacation each August when we visited Grandma for a week. We went to the show, swam and visited with all the relatives before returning home to work and wait for next summer.

Because we worked together, we enjoyed playing together with an intensity unknown today. Our family became a very close group and still is today. Now all the children are grown and 10 grandchildren have rounded out our family. Dad is retired and enjoying life, and we make the rounds visiting with the children and their families. Summer brings visits from the grandchildren, who help us with the garden and go fishing and camping with us, and time goes on and on.

In retrospect I sometimes long for those bygone days. Despite the hard work, long hours and going without, I do have fond memories of those days of the farm.

Winnie Schuetz
Tilden, Illinois

■

Chapter 6: Natural Catastrophes

Summers in the 1930s

Summer months in the 1930s meant hot, dry temperatures. My parents and I lived on a 100-acre farm in eastern Nebraska.

Clouds of huge, two- and three-inch yellow-striped grass-hoppers were arriving daily as they flew in from the southern states, where they had already consumed available crops. They were settling in on local pastures and fields to feast.

Feed stores quickly stocked up on ingredients for a poison that had to be mixed fresh each morning to be used by farmers. It would stick onto the dewy crops, pasture grass or edges of hay-fields when used this way.

At 7 years of age, I was dressed to help, wearing overalls, a long-sleeved shirt and a large-brimmed straw hat securely tied under my chin.

Dad's team of horses, Tom and Jerry, was hitched to our farm wagon and away we drove out to the fields, with the poisoned mixture that smelled like bran and banana oil. On our arrival down a dusty lane, Dad used a shovel to toss the mixture onto the edges of our pasture, the end cornrows and hayfields. This proce-dure was repeated several times a week.

As the horses slowly pulled the wagon in the designated areas, swarms of grasshoppers would cling onto clothing and spit a liquid like tobacco juice, making me scream.

Car windows had to be kept closed even in the 90- to 100-degree heat as hoppers attempted to fly into the car as you drove the dusty country roads.

After coming into the house from the awful trip and taking a quick bath, Mama would announce that it was nice weather to make root beer.

Together we collected long-necked glass bottles for that purpose. While the bottles were washed and sterilized, then set to cool, my job began. Standing on a low stool next to the cabinet, I used the long mixing spoon to stir the mixture of water, Hires root beer extract from a square bottle and sugar in our largest canning kettle. A yeast mixture was then added and after thoroughly stirred, it was funneled into the bottles. Each bottle was filled a half-inch from the top with root beer mixture. Dad, using bottle caps from a box marked 12 dozen, carefully placed a cap on each. The capper attached and sealed the caps tightly on several dozen bottles. They were then carried to our summer kitchen and placed on their sides in a shady area. For three days they were rolled and turned to different positions to mix the ingredients. After that they were carried down the 23 steps to our deep cave to chill.

About a week later we sampled the cold fizzing root beer, and any visitors got cold mugs of this delicious drink. Some batches were not drunk up quickly, and the root beer would get powerful. Mom would have me come outdoors, and in order not to waste any, she would have me hold a large clean aluminum bucket at chest level at an angle. When she removed the cap, she could aim that forceful stream of root beer into the bucket. I was often dowsed with the sticky stuff, and I got many a mouthful of root beer that way!

> Rita M. Grashorn
> Fremont, Nebraska

Midwest Weather

Weather dominated our life, being a prime topic of conversation and indeed the aura that orchestrated our existence. My uncle's diary entries reported the temperature, the direction of the wind in the morning, as well as any changes during the day.

The seasons were distinct. Spring scarcely appeared when the earth suddenly warmed in May and one felt that "God's in His heaven, all's right with the world." Dad with horses and plow was in the field and the clear, sparkling song of the meadowlarks punctuated the air. School was out in mid-May, and soon we were catapulted into the season of storms, with crashing thunder and spectacular lightning. Dad always watched the clouds, and as a darkening sky threatened a tornado he closed the barn door and hustled us with wraps and flashlight down into the cave. He stayed near the top steps, and only after the wind became furious would he close the slanting door. Our farm was spared, but I remember visiting the shambles where a tornado had struck.

Summers were humid and often got up to 100 degrees. We often retreated to the basement to pit cherries, peel apples and do other chores preparatory to canning.

Fall was corn picking time. With horses and wagon Dad worked the rows, husking and heaving the ears up against the sideboard and into the wagon. Each bang resounded in the crisp fall air. As the trees lost their leaves their configuration stood in stark relief with a beauty of their own.

Winter brought snow and severity. Dad changed the wagon wheels to sleigh runners; it was our transportation to and from school two miles away. At times he bedded us down under horse blankets, kneeled in the wagon with his fur-lined coat, collar up, cap with earflaps, reins over his shoulder as he drove the horses.

Early spring was a time of rains, cloudbursts and swollen creeks. Dad would take us to school in the buggy or carriage, the narrow wheels slicing the mud as he hummed his monotonous though comforting melody.

Nature's voice was our companion, the cosmos in which we lived. Though nature often disciplined us harshly, again she was sweet and loving. We tuned our lives to her authority, and in her rhythms experienced both confinement and enhancement.

Bernice Severson
Portland, Oregon

How Did We Survive?

You know I guess I could write a book about life on the farm as I have always lived on a farm and I am now 81 years old.

From 1934, when we got married, there were so many hard times. The dry weather, the grasshoppers, milking the cows and raising chickens and hogs so you could earn a living. We worked for a farmer in 1935 for $30 a month, a house to live in and milk and eggs. We bought a Model A Roadster and paid $15 a month for it.

We started to farm for ourselves in 1936. The dry weather and grasshoppers got our first crop. We had to mow the oat crop to have something to feed our cows. We sold eggs and cream each week to buy our groceries and gas for our car to go home and back to town the next week. There was no electricity or water in the house. How did we survive?

Anna L. Lammers
Red Cloud, Nebraska

My First Dust Storm

In 1934 I helped my sister, Hazel Hoien, at Mound, North Dakota, where she was teaching school. We had letters from Conde, South Dakota, telling of dust storms but could not visualize them. We were where the rolling hills and grassland kept the dust at a minimum. School was out and we took the train to Aberdeen where the folks met us. Both of us noticed that there were loose ridges of dust along the road but we were really amazed when we got in the house and saw heavy dust in the window sills and corners everywhere. It crossed our minds that maybe Mother had let up on her housekeeping.

Hazel was to be married in June to Lyle Overby. We knew there was a lot of cleaning to do at the church, but first Hazel and I went to work at home with soap and water and small brushes to clean out all of the dust. We put a lot of elbow grease into it and finally decided the place was clean enough.

Two days later, about noon, Father came to the house and said, "A dust storm is coming!" I went out on the back porch, and there to the northwest was a wall of roiling dust reaching high into the heavens and to the right and left as far as I could see. Mother called me to come and help. Sheets and blankets were soaked in water and wrung out to hang over doors and windows. The storm hit before they were all covered but we kept at the job. The wind was strong and I hoped it would soon blow itself out. Each time anyone went outside, billows of dust entered the house. We gasped and coughed. Mother had put some food out for lunch before the storm hit and now we looked at the table and saw that it was all covered with a fine silt. The pattern in the oilcloth was completely obscured. The wind howled, the dust came in and there was nothing to do but endure it. Father put a cloth over his mouth and nose and went out to take care of the animals. When he came in, his whisker stubble, eyebrows and all around his eyes was covered with dust. He was choking and coughing.

I don't recall our supper that night. I know I asked the folks how long the storm would last and they said, "Until the wind dies down." I wanted to go to bed, but the dust was so thick on the comforter that you could hardly see the pattern of the pieces. Where could you take it to shake it out? There was more dust outside where this had come from. We removed the top quilts and tried to sleep, but each time we moved a cloud of dust would strangle us.

This dust storm, my first, began at about 11 a.m. and continued unabated until around 6 a.m. the next day. When the skies finally cleared we saw drifts all around the farm buildings. Father had to shovel the dirt away from the back door where it had drifted up on it. We began to clean house and shake out bedding but we certainly realized fast that one going over could not clean it completely. In later storms the fence rows filled so cattle could walk right over the top.

Eunice Hoien Dahlgren
Sweet Home, Oregon

"We Couldn't See Our Hands in Front of Our Faces"

Dear Cuz,

My turn to write so here goes. This day started out real sunny. The mile we walk to school is really nice, especially when we leave a little early. We can watch the ants move from one house to another and name all the flowers we see on the way. Vern made a mistake, he put his lunch down while we watched the ants and halfway to school he discovered he was carrying a sackful of them. He decided to let them have it so he took his apple out and threw the sack in the pasture. He didn't go hungry though, for we all shared some of our lunch. He probably got more to eat then the other five of us who shared with him.

About two this afternoon we noticed another dust storm approaching from the north. Three layers this time: first layer light, next layer reddish and third layer black. Vern decided we'd better go home or Mom would worry. The rest of the kids stayed at school till it blew over or someone came to pick them up. The six of us and Alice and Raymond, our neighbors, went out and climbed through the fence into the pasture and walked single file along the fence. Halfway home the sand hit us in the face. We all joined hands and hung on tight and walked close to the barbed-wire fence. Vern led and Raymond brought up the rear; they were the oldest and biggest. When we got to the corner we climbed through the fence and took a head count, even though we couldn't see our hands in front of our faces. We crossed the road through our gate still holding hands and marched into the house. When we got into the house Mom, who was busy wetting the sheets to hang over the doors and windows, was glad to see us.

That's why we have cream-colored sheets. No white ones. We're really in fashion these days. Really uptown we are. Of course all our neighbors have the same color sheets on their clotheslines.

After the dust quit blowing the neighbors walked the last half mile to their house.

When they left I went in and washed the sand off the dishes

before setting the table for supper. After we eat I'll go shake the bedding out so we won't have to sleep in the sand. Tomorrow before school I'll dust and hope there are no more dust storms for a while—three or four a week is a little much.

Well Cuz, nothing new around here except some new white kittens, so best sign my John Henry.

With loads of love your cousin, Mae.

Mae C. Reed

Aztec, New Mexico

Droughts and Floods in the '30s

My grandpa, George Weeden, came to Cheyenne County, Kansas, around 1893 in a covered wagon. He established a homestead and built a sod house. He brought his family out later. Then he built a rock barn, chicken house and milk house. Down the hill he gave land for a school. I was born in 1930, the fifth child of six children. I always look back to my farm home with pleasure. I know my parents went through hard times but they did the best they could and we were happy.

The dirt storm years were bad. Some days the chickens went to roost at 3:00 in the afternoon because it was so dark from the blowing dust. My parents argued over the weather; Dad wanted it to rain so bad he would see a little cloud and say it looked like rain, while Mom would say it never rained from that direction. Mom was usually right. The crops and pastures dried up and still there was no rain. Then, on Memorial Day 1935, it rained and rained, so much so that we had to hold rags in the windows to keep the water out. The next day we heard on the phone that the river had flooded, so we got in the car and went to see. I can still remember a dead cow hung on a corner of the bridge, and the roiling, dirty water carrying dishes and pans roaring by. Several people drowned, and we were at a neighbors' when they brought in some survivors we knew.

Mrs. Alvin Holzworth

St. Francis, Kansas

Prayer Saved Us from the Tornado

My grandfather, Soren C. Anderson, received the "patent papers" on his land donation claim September 29th, 1888. They are signed by President Grover Cleveland, and entitled him to 153 and 99/100th acres. It was not a full quarter section of 160 acres because the land was just five miles from the "correction line." Grandpa raised wheat and corn, as well as some cattle and hogs. After a number of years he began to buy up nearby land until he had four additional quarter sections.

This is how it came about that in 1911 my father, John Hoien, rented two quarter sections from my grandfather. The land was about six miles west of Conde, South Dakota. I was born on that farm in 1914. We had a large, two-story L-shaped house with a roofed side porch filling in the L. Our barn was only a small shed but when I was 4 years old a large barn with a big haymow was built. One day when it was nearly finished, I was playing in the yard, barefooted, when my father called to me, saying, "Go and wash your feet real good in the horse trough." I did and Father came and carried me to the new cement that had been poured for the driveway between the stalls in the barn. He carefully set me down in the wet cement, with his hand pressing my feet deep into it. When he lifted me up he said I could wash my feet again. So my footprints were always there in the barn. I was quite proud of them and when other children came to play with us I'd take them to the barn to show off my footprints.

It was about a year later on a dry, extremely hot summer day that we saw black clouds forming in the northwest. Soon Father came running to the house shouting, "A tornado is coming!" He then hurried to the barn to close the big haymow door. Mother gathered us children into a back bedroom where we clung to her. We could hear the awful rumble of the wind that shook the ground as the funnel approached. Although it was daytime it became very dark, and I remember Mother quietly praying for God to protect us. Suddenly there was a screeching, grinding sound, the house shook and then all became quiet and rain began to fall. We looked out and Father came, saying it was all past now. Then we saw that the corner porch post had been wrenched out of our side porch! There were five buildings on our farm and that was the only damage to any of them. One header box had been lifted off of its wheels and smashed, and we found a few dead chickens, but we all felt that God had heard Mother's prayers for protection.

Eunice Hoien Dahlgren
Sweet Home Oregon

Chapter 7: Animals Close to Our Hearts

The Orphan Rabbits

On the farm many unusual things happened with dogs and other animals. Our dog once caught and killed a mother rabbit. Our dad saw it and realized she had left behind two tiny babies. He caught them and carried them home in his coat pocket. He gave them to us kids. We soon had a box all ready for them. They ate oatmeal and plenty of green grass. We took good care of them and they were real pets.

Rabbits grow fast and soon they could get out of the box. We would have to go and look for them, finding them hiding in a corner or under the beds.

When our dad played the accordion our rabbits would come and listen to him play. As animals do they soon grew too big to keep in the house so their nesting box was moved outdoors. Our dog knew they were pets so never did bother them. We could still pick them up and hold them, but they were harder and harder to catch. One day we realized we had not seen our pets for several days.

Sometime later, on a Sunday evening, Dad sat on the porch playing his accordion. He called to us to come and see. There inside the yard sat our two rabbits. The music had brought them home again.

Myrtle Barker
Monmouth, Oregon

Little Bess and Queen

Sometime in the late spring after the winter of the big ice, which was 1936 and '37, Dad came home from a farm sale with this little bay mare. He said I could have her if I wanted her. What better offer could a 10-year-old boy ever get? Boy! A horse of my very own.

The owner's wife's name was Bessie, so the mare became Bess. Somewhere along the line the word little was attached to her name and she became Little Bess.

She should have been a sorrel, but her mane and tail were black and her legs were dark, which made her a bay. She was not at all pretty but I thought her to be the most beautiful horse in all Missouri.

I broke her to ride. She was a very fast walker who would run her heart out for you. She weighed just over 900 pounds. I once rode her 11 miles in 45 minutes.

We built a cart from parts of an old buggy. Every boy in the neighborhood rode around with me but most of the girls were not interested. I wasn't interested in them either.

I rode Little Bess everywhere and couldn't stay off of her. She was my dream come true. Mom said it was hard to get me off to come eat.

When I started high school Dad thought I needed a better horse so he came up with a full-blooded Arabian that I called "Queen." She was the first horse I ever rode that would "neck rein" and the only horse I ever rode that had a gait called "single foot." It gave you a smooth ride that covered ground in a hurry.

We lived east of town, and a girl who lived west of town needed a horse to ride to school. We sold Little Bess to her. This was during World War II, when you couldn't get gasoline, but all we needed was oats.

Every school day for the next two years Little Bess and Queen stood side by side in a stall just three blocks from the schoolhouse.

That was when I first became interested in girls. I still wonder if I wasn't more interested in the way the girl cared for Little Bess than I was in her.

I finished high school and the girl dropped out after two years. I kept Queen until she died of old age, but whatever became of Little Bess or the girl is more than I know.

H. Dean Yearns
Queen City, Missouri

Unwelcome Pets

The usual farm family had an assorted number of cats and dogs along with other selected animals. One of our favorite pets that I recall was Old Bud, our Shetland pony. He always seemed old to me and was a bit stubborn. On occasion he pulled us to school in the buggy, along with some of the neighbor kids. I recall one day my oldest sister was riding him to the field where Dad was working. When it was necessary to cross a stream he decided he didn't want to, so he laid down in the middle with the rider on his back. He had found too much corn to eat at one time, and his hooves were grown out and curved up, making it difficult to walk. It was necessary for him to stand in mud or water several hours or even days to soften his hooves so Dad could trim them.

Buster was one dog among many that we had. I recall my brother poured kerosene on his back and he lost all his hair—he was not a pretty dog!

Another pet was not a very welcomed one by Mom. Robert and I were playing in the corncrib when we saw some cute little black-and-white kittens coming from beneath the floor—he caught one and took it to the house to share with Mom. Her surprised comment was, "Get that skunk out of here!" The mother skunk had been destroyed a day or two before when she was found helping herself to the chickens; apparently her babies were getting hungry and had come out looking for her.

Margaret Blair
Lorimor, Iowa

God, My Husband and Lady

I was rushing out of the feed store, eager to get home when I heard her...

"Whee... eee... eee... eee!"

I turned to see this darling little filly. She was a feed store demonstration, displayed in a small fenced-in area in the parking lot. Never in my wildest dreams did I think that God would use this horse to bring my husband to such a close relationship with him!

I kept telling myself it seemed cruel and inhumane to keep this animal penned up in a four-by-nine spot. I couldn't resist walking up to her. Her soft, warm nuzzle against my bare arm that hot summer day almost made me cry!

"Hi! You're a pretty lady!" I said, patting her head. She immediately responded with a series of nickers and neighs that seemed to say: "Buy me... eee... eee... eee..." I hurried home and tried to go about my business as usual, but somehow I kept hearing an echo in my thoughts:

"Love me... eee... eee..."

My husband, Emmitt, loves horses. One thing I had discovered in my wonderful marriage was that Emmitt had a very tender spot for animals.

I took Emmitt to see Lady and he fell for her right on the spot. She had the same effect on him that she had on me.

Since we lived at the edge of town and had an acre of backyard, we thought she would be easier to care for there than on our small farm. Even though Emmitt would not admit to how much he cared for the horse, I would catch him talking to her from the window. Then he would go outside and let her chase him.

Lady was a privileged character and she knew it. She would run around inside the yard with the dogs and frolic playfully.

"Oh no!" I said one day. "She thinks she's a dog! Look... she is chasing cars with them!" Our animals were safely enclosed inside a chain link fence, but they would run up and down the fence every time a car went by.

As we loved and laughed and enjoyed our playful filly, we

noticed one day that Lady was growing into a very beautiful animal. Since we had quarter horse papers on her, Emmitt boasted to the neighbors that we had to spell in front of her, because she didn't know that she was a horse!

As she turned into a lovely yearling, Emmitt warned me:

"Use caution. She wouldn't intend to hurt you, but she's mighty frisky."

Emmitt had to have surgery that winter and I had to feed Lady until he was able to be up and around. We got along fine, except for one cold, brisk morning.

"Look, it snowed last night," I exclaimed, opening the shutters. "And look at Lady. She's waiting for her breakfast!" Lady was standing at her trough in her shed, pawing at the ground impatiently.

I just slipped my coat on over my pajamas and hurried out. The glistening snow sparkled in the sun. The soft crunch under my boots made deep imprints in the newly fallen snow. I fed Lady and she was munching happily. As I started to walk back to the house, Emmitt's warning suddenly came to mind.

"Don't let her know you're afraid of her," he would say.

Feeling uneasy, I felt the urge to run backwards so I could keep her in my sight. She caught on that I was fearful, and here she came, running, kicking and bucking! Every time I would start for the house, she would head me off. I ran and jumped on top of the woodpile and there I sat!

"This is ridiculous," I thought. "Me, a grown woman out here in my pajamas, because I'm being intimidated by a horse!"

Finally Emmitt looked out the window, called to her and I made a run for it! I made it in two seconds!

Summer came and she ate everything that grew through the chain link fence and everything she could reach over it—rose bushes, trees, nothing was safe within her reach!

I finally persuaded Emmitt to take her to the farm, and although he didn't have as much time to spend with her, my yard improved considerably.

Lady loved her new freedom at the farm. What a thrilling sight she was. Head and tail held high, running like the wind! I would watch her and think about the many times I had taken the beautiful things God has created for granted. And then it happened. I could tell from Emmitt's face as he walked in the door one day that he was hurting deep inside.

"Lady's suddenly gone lame," he said dejectedly. "I can't figure out what happened. She was all right yesterday. I had the vet out. He cannot find anything wrong!"

I will admit that there had been times when I had been a wee bit jealous of Lady, but the thought of her hopping around on three legs made my heart ache too!

After all of the shots, liniment rubs and anxious moments of three weeks, she was still no better.

I am always amazed at God's perfect timing. A friend "just so happened" to loan me a tape. It was about a man who had prayed for his horse and the horse got well.

We listened intently to the tape, and I discovered that God cares about what we care about, even animals.

"Come on," Emmitt jumped up shouting. "We're going to the farm right now and pray for Lady!"

It was a balmy summer night. The moonlight seemed to be shining on Lady in a special way, and all of us seemed to sense the awesome beauty and wonder of God. A myriad of stars twinkled, and the distant cooing of doves made everything so peaceful.

Lady nickered to us in her usual way as we walked up to her. She put her velvety soft nose against Emmitt's shirt and stood on three legs, motionless.

I began to sob as Emmitt poured out his heart to God.

"Thank You Lord," he was saying. "Thank You for allowing me to know how real You are. Whether You heal Lady or not, my life will never be the same and how I praise You for that!"

From that moment on, I had a brand new husband! He awakened the next morning with a new zest for living, grateful for everything in this wonderful world our wonderful God has made.

I could hardly wait to get to the farm the next day. When we drove up, there was Lady, still hobbling around on three legs.

"I don't care if Lady is crippled the rest of her life," Emmitt exclaimed, "I praise God for everything! No use keeping Lady shut up like this. I'll open the gate—at least maybe she can limp around and eat a little green grass."

The instant Emmitt opened the gate, something seemed to quicken in Lady. She shot out of that gate so fast, her head and tail up high! She started running like the wind!

There was never a racing thoroughbred any more beautiful! She galloped the full length of the pasture and back to us on four strong, beautiful, lovely legs!

It was then that I looked at my husband. Tears were streaming down his face and his arms were raised to heaven in thanksgiving! Not only had God answered Emmitt's prayer for Lady, He had answered my prayer for Emmitt!

We still have Lady. She foaled last spring... a darling little colt!

Many people have wanted to buy Lady, but my husband just smiles and says: "She's not for sale. She's a very unusual horse. God meant her just for me. Let me tell you about it!"

Joan Clayton
Portales, New Mexico

Feisty and Slinky

When I was growing up on a farm in Iowa, my favorite farm animals were Feisty the rooster and Slinky the cat. Slinky was a black-and-white cat who got his name from the way he stalked his prey. I have a picture of me petting Slinky and holding Feisty.

Feisty was quite a pet. He just loved to crow. However, one day he quit crowing. We couldn't figure out what was wrong with him. He didn't seem to be sick. After several weeks, Dad decided maybe we should butcher him. When we dressed him, we found out he (or she) was just about ready to lay eggs. Dad figured that must have been why he quit crowing.

Joy J. Palmer
Forest City, Iowa

Never Afraid with Tommy

In the '30s my folks lived on two different farms just three miles north of Denver.

I was 10 or 11 when my dad would turn old Bossie and her yearling heifer calf out on the country road to graze all day. Towards evening she would head back home, but to hurry her up, I would have to go after her. After a few tries, I had gotten Daisy the heifer tamed so I could get on and ride her home.

Later, when I was 12 to 18, I worked in the fields with Dad until dark most days. After work, I would leave to walk a mile or so out in the pasture for the four or five milk cows. I always took my big, old yellow tomcat. He would follow along meowing and talking to me as we went. At times he would stop and sniff a gopher hole. Then, all of a sudden, he would come running past me, and then stop to wait for me. I don't know why, but I was never afraid of the dark as long as I had Tommy with me.

Theresa Stingerie Bainbridge
La Salle, Colorado

The Proud Mother Hen

In the springtime our white Leghorn chickens would be ready to set. A nest of up to 15 eggs was made ready for these hens. In three weeks small, yellow fluffy chickens pecked their way out of the eggshells. Their downy feathers were so soft to touch. They soon grew, with the soft fluff being replaced by feathers.

Wild Mallard ducks nested each year near our grain field. On one occasion our dog caught and killed a mother duck who was on her nest. Our dad rescued the eggs and brought them home. They were put under a setting hen. In due time they hatched. Mother Hen was so proud of her family and was soon able to take them out into the farmyard.

The young ducklings realized there was a pond nearby and were soon swimming merrily. Poor Mother Hen stood on the shores "clucking" for her brood. The young ducks were happy until dusk and then were glad to return to their Mother Hen and their nesting box. This continued day after day, with the Mother Hen waiting for her family to come to her.

The ducks grew and soon Mother Hen let them go to the pond alone while she stayed in the yard with the chickens.

Myrtle Barker
Monmouth, Oregon

Precious Peeper

One year our geese didn't earn any college money for me. We hatched the eggs in incubators. I did everything I was supposed to do, including keeping the eggs at the right temperature and turning them over daily. The eggs would develop right up to a week before time to hatch. Then they would suddenly die and rot. We couldn't figure out what was the matter. Then a thought occurred to us one day. The breeding stock geese had been kept in the lot where the cattle were several years before. The cattle had been fed diethylstilbestrol. We asked the veterinarian if that could be the cause of our problem, since the geese like to drill their beaks into mud puddles. The veterinarian said he couldn't say for sure. That was before the harmful effects of DES were known. After that, we kept the geese out of that area and didn't have any more trouble.

That year only one gosling hatched out of 360 eggs. She was really spoiled. We named her Peeper because she sounded like a robin when she was little. We kept her in a cardboard box in the kitchen until she got bigger. When she grew up, we kept her for breeding stock for several years. Even when she was older she would answer me with a "Cock, cock, cock" when I would call to her from the house. Sometimes she would come running to see what I wanted.

Joy J. Palmer
Forest City, Iowa

Goats Were Part of Growing Up

Growing up on a small farm, I still have warm memories of some of the various animals who shared that life. Quite possibly that accounts for my love and concern for animals today.

Some friends once gave my dad and mother a pair of young goats. We had never had goats before, so all of us were very proud and excited to have them. The names we gave them, Billy and Nannie, of course fell right into place. You guessed it, they soon became big pets and followed us all over when we were outside. That was definitely to our liking, and a few days of our indulging and talking to them made them think they were a pair of VIGs.

How excited we were later when Mama and Papa told us Billy and Nannie had become proud parents of a tiny kid. I do believe a baby goat is one of the sweetest and most cuddly of all little animals. We promptly named her Betty Lou.

That was just before Christmas, and we had just gotten out of school for two weeks of vacation when a big snow came. It gets much colder in southwestern Mississippi than here in Houston, but to have a solid white, thick hard-packed layer of snow cover the ground and stay there for two whole weeks is a rarity even there.

Since Betty Lou was a newborn, she had to be brought into the house to keep her from freezing. Mama made a bed for her in a cardboard box and put her against the back of the chimney in one of the bedrooms. The fire in the living room kept the back of the chimney warm. We didn't have central heat on the farm in those days, so all of us hovered near the fireplace in freezing weather.

Nannie, who was in the barn, was led around to the back porch by the bedroom and Betty Lou was taken outside for her feedings, then brought back inside to her warm bed. What a Christmas vacation we had that year! We held Betty Lou, loved and cuddled her, and pampered her as much as any three two-legged kids ever could have one four-legged kid.

Finally the snow melted. Betty Lou was put outside again, and we went back to school.

Betty Lou grew, and in time the herd of goats also grew. We still liked them, but they were not quite the novelty they had been at first, although we still gave some of them names.

One day Mama told us Papa had decided to butcher Sam, one of the young male goats. What a squawk we put up over that! Finally Mama told us if Papa didn't butcher Sam, it would probably be Betty Lou. That was such a horrible thought that it definitely put an end to all of our fussing right then and there.

Being young then, with a hard and cold heart, I thoroughly enjoyed the nice steaks and roasts from Sam. Years later though, when visiting my sister-in-law Lorraine and her family on their farm in Missouri, I took on the job of feeding her baby lamb who had lost his mother. He was so cute and greedy, and as I would sit on the back steps and give him his bottle, milk would spatter all over. She mentioned selling him for money for a trip to Chicago. When I protested, my mother-in-law said I would never make a farmer's wife, since I would never sell nor butcher any of the animals. She was probably right.

Billy, Nannie, Betty Lou and the rest of the goats spent a good many years on the farm. Goats are very clean animals that eat mostly the leaves from bushes. They kept the undergrowth cleaned out, and we had milk many times.

Finally Billy began to get mean, and he especially seemed to have it in for Mama. He would try to slip up behind her and butt her with his horns, which were quite long by then. Mama kept worrying and fussing about him, and we all became a little wary when we were outside around him.

One day Mama went out to the chicken house to gather the eggs. It wasn't a very strong house, but it served the chickens adequately. Billy saw her go inside and close the door behind her. He went over and started to butt the door, one time after another. He was quite large and strong, and would rear up on his hind legs and come down against the door with a bang. He would soon have broken the door, and since he knew he had her trapped inside, would either have hurt her badly or killed her. Lucky for Mama, Papa heard her screams and came on the run.

After that Billy's days on the farm were numbered. He learned too late that you should never butt the hand that feeds you. Everyone, even Mama, was a little sad, but since he could no longer be trusted, he simply had to go. He probably ended up on the butcher block, but he brought about his own undoing.

Papa eventually sold all of the goats, but I remember them as a very important part of my growing-up years.

Bessie Aspan
Houston, Texas

The Pet Bull Calf

We lived on a farm for a couple of years during the Second World War. Our father had died several years before. Three brothers and a brother-in-law were off to war and five of us younger kids were at home. Our 16-year-old brother had an old Model A car that he was always tinkering with. He was our only transportation. We all helped rock that car out of ditches.

The first spring we were there was one of those very wet ones; all the bottoms were covered with water. My sister was watching for this one cow to calve. When she did, she led it across the pasture and it fell off into a ravine that was beginning to fill. Martha got that baby out of the edge of the water and carried it back to the barn. She made a pet out of that little bull calf. During the same wet spell, lightning struck a tree and killed seven head of cattle, which I can still remember being swept away!

Jane Shepard Dungy
Stewartsville, Missouri

Rooster with a Mean Streak

I was raised on a farm, and I married a farmer. I had two sons: a 7-year-old and a baby. My parents were raising a granddaughter, my sister's child, who was the same age as my older son.

My parents had a big, old red rooster with a mean streak. The rooster would flog the granddaughter at every opportunity, but never offered to bother my older son when we visited. Maybe the rooster sensed that 7-year-old boys are much braver than 7-year-old girls.

My parents decided to give the rooster to my older son, and all went well until the baby was old enough to play in the sandbox in our backyard. One afternoon I heard my younger son scream, and I knew exactly what was happening. I ran for the back door, but our family dog, Pandy, was already at the baby's side attacking that old rooster. I clapped my hands and yelled "Sick 'em, Pandy, sick 'em!"

Pandy didn't kill that mean old rooster that day, but she sure gave him a tussle. She must have proven her point, because the rooster never attacked anyone again.

Margie Van Meter
Lewistown, Missouri

Easter Bunnies

Money was hard to come by in the early '30s and it was getting close to Easter time.

I knew that I had plenty of eggs to boil for the children's Easter egg hunt, and I could use beet juice and other juices to color, but I wanted to get them some candy eggs. It would be such a treat for them and they didn't ask for much.

Then I happened to think—I had just taken 30 baby rabbits away from their mothers. I wondered if I could sell them for Easter bunnies.

I got busy and made a nice sign and put it out by the road in front of the house. I put the price at 75 cents. I was surprised. In three days I had sold them all! $10.50! Wow, I felt like the richest woman in town. That was a lot of money in those days.

I was not only able to get some candy for the children but was able to buy things we might not have had for our Easter dinner.

Evelyn Williams-Hall
Sioux City, Iowa

Dressed Hams

One summer afternoon, two little girls had nothing to do. Delores suggested, "Let's play dolls with the new little pigs."

Susan replied, "Well, I don't know if Grandma would like that. And..." she stammered, "I am kind of afraid of that big mama pig."

Delores said, "Well, that old sow won't hurt a flea, scaredy-cat! Come on, sissy."

"Well, OK."

They ran indoors, packing Susan's little suitcase to the brim with new doll clothes that her aunt in Chicago had made for her. Running, she caught up with Delores, who already was crawling into the little hut tacked to the back of the barn where the big, old white China sow lay on her side dozing as her little piglets suckled her warm, nutritious milk. Susan quickly crawled into the tiny enclosure. She reached behind her to close the wee door.

Delores reached for a little pig and tossed it gently into Susan's lap. She then took another one from Mama Sow's faucet to make room for two more piglets to get their turn. Susan unsnapped the suitcase and removed a green silk dress and matching baby bonnet. Delores pawed through it to the bottom, finding a cute white pinafore with cherry blossoms scattered over it. The girls busied themselves with pulling tiny front legs through the puffed sleeves of the dress. Susan laid the little pig she was playing with on its back as she carefully tied the jade bonnet under his chin. Then she reached once more into the far corner of the suitcase. Searching there, she found a pretty little pink pair of bloomers. These she deftly slipped onto her little pig's hindquarters. Pulling the hind legs through the bloomer legs, Delores again rummaged through the clothes until she found a tiny doll's shawl, which she fastened around her little pig's neck. From time to time she stopped to reach over to pat and scratch Mama Sow on her side or snout. The girls played for about an hour trying all the dresses on their little doll-like pigs, which did not seem to mind. It became very hot and humid in the cramped quarters. The girls soon tired of the fun and repacked the suitcase, returning their pig-dolls to Mama Sow for a snack. The girls crawled out of the lean-to and fastened the door securely. As they wandered down the gravel path back to the house Susan said, "Gee, baby pigs' high fashion silks are cute. We did have a good time."

Many years later Susan related this story to her mother. She was informed how very lucky she and Delores had been. Her mother said, "It was a good thing that every animal on Gramp's farm was a pet. You and Dee might have been chased or killed and even eaten by Mama Sow. It was fun, but it could have turned out to be a real tragedy. Children should always tell their elders where they are going and what they are going to do." On that summer afternoon no one saw the girls crawl into the house and no one knew they were there.

Crescence Stadeble
DeKalb, Illinois

Susie the Goose

It seemed like every animal we had on our small farm sooner or later became a pet. They gave us lots of laughs and joy.

Susie was a very adventuresome goose, generally into everything on the place. In the morning she waited on the back step for me to come out and followed me everywhere she could.

Susie had plenty of places where she could get water, as our chickens and geese ran out and were not always in the pen. One day Susie decided she wanted a drink so she headed for the cows' barrel. The water was lower than usual, and as she bent to get a drink she fell in. How she did sputter. After getting out she was so mad she chased the chickens all over the place. It was quite funny.

The children had been playing in the garden space and had dug a hole. It rained that night, and of course in the morning Susie went out to investigate. She slipped in the hole and how she sputtered. My 5-year-old laughed at her and Susie started to chase him. We really did enjoy our funny goose, Susie, and her antics.

Evelyn Williams-Hall
Sioux City, Iowa

Our Cat

Down on the farm we had a variety of pets and animals. Each spring a new batch of fluffy kittens was born at the barn. We watched them grow and even persuaded our mom to let us have one as a house cat. He was such a gentle animal. We girls dressed him in doll clothes we had made, even a bonnet. When he grew tired of our game he jumped from our lap to the floor, waited for us to undress him and headed for the door.

My sister always said that he said "me out" and not "meow" when he wanted out.

Myrtle Barker
Monmouth, Oregon

Blackberry, the Queen of the Cows

My parents went into farming when I was 7. They started off with a dairy. There was an odd assortment of cows: Guernsey, Holstein and Jersey. The product of one of these cows and a non-dairy bull was a blotched black heifer named Blackberry. She became a haughty cow who seemed to think she was a bit better than the other members of the herd. Blackberry stayed clean while the other cows got muddy. She seemed to have the best stalks of hay and the sunniest spot on a cold day.

It was a disturbing day when we found her down and unable to get up. She continued to chew her cud and looked as if she was resting, but nothing could get her up. We had to bring her food and water. She was 8 years old. She still maintained her dignified air even though she could not stand.

My dad figured out a way to slide her around. He moved her to a more sheltered spot near the stock trailer. The vet didn't know what ailed Blackberry, so he didn't know what to do for her. The thought had come more than once that her life should be ended, except that she didn't appear to be in pain. This situation lasted for one or two months.

Then one morning Daddy was in a hurry to use the stock trailer. He connected it to the pickup and pulled away too fast. Suddenly, he remembered Blackberry. He stopped the pickup and hurried over to see if she was okay.

Evidently, the commotion had startled Blackberry. She stood on wobbly legs. What ailed Blackberry was never known. From that day on, she could walk. There was no monetary loss of a good cow, and there was no sentimental loss of an almost pet. The monarch returned to reigning over her domain.

Jonette Shuja
Mount Prospect, Illinois

———■———

Chapter 8: Simple Pleasures

The Player Piano

Our family had one home entertainment musical instrument in the late '20s and '30s that none of our neighbors had—a player piano. It sat in the parlor waiting to be played, ever ready for someone to sit right down and pump out a tune. It was an upright Gulbransen, and the bench was large enough to seat three people: the operator and one on each side. Quite often there was more than one enjoying the music. The rolls were kept in the bench under the lid or seat, which lifted up providing good storage space. We had a variety of rolls that were easy to insert, and then the operator started pumping the foot pedals and presto—there was beautiful piano music with the words to songs alongside the roll. Ninety percent of the music played was accompanied by the pumper vocally and by anyone else nearby.

Oh if I had the wings of an angel
Over these prison walls I would fly
And I'd fly to the arms of my poor darlin'
And there I'd be willing to die.

Playing the player piano was one of my favorite pastimes, and I loved to sing along with the music. How convenient it was to be an instant musician and vocalist.

Valencia—In my arms I held your charms
Beneath the starry skies above—
Valencia—In my dreams it always seems I
Hear you softly calling to me...

Quite often Mom mail-ordered clothing and other materials

from Sears and Wards, and it seemed that with almost every order she would buy new rolls. We kids always looked forward to the new additions to our "repertoire."

Collegiate—Collegiate—Yes we are Collegiate
Nothing intermediate—We're Collegiate, RAH, RAH, RAH!

As we kids grew older and entered our teens, we were allowed to have parties at our house that were attended by neighborhood kids. What a workout the player piano got. Of course we played games like they do at all parties, but it wasn't long until there was a crowd around the piano, and everyone joined in the singing.

Today's kids would probably think what a dull party, but we had good clean fun, and it didn't matter whether one was a good singer or not. I think Mom enjoyed these parties as much as we kids, and she always served one of her super good lunches.

During the winter months the parlor door was shut to conserve fuel, and the piano got a rest. We didn't have central heating, consequently it was cold in that room most of the time, except for a few warm days when Mom would open the door to let some heat into the room—then it was back to the piano.

Grownups also enjoyed the piano, but not like we young people. When there was a party at our house for the grownups, they did play a few rolls and they would dance. I have a feeling they thought the player part was more for the younger people and group singing.

We had one roll that was, as far as I was concerned, more like a military march. There were no words to it and the title was "The Jolly Coppersmith." Our Grandpa Hager, little old German that he was, seemed to consider it more of a dance tune. If he was visiting our house and one of us was playing "The Jolly Coppersmith" he'd go into his "frenzy" of a dance. It's hard to explain, but I'll try. He would dance alone, and such foot stomping and whirling you never saw before. Our mother was always glad when his dancing was over, and I remember once she asked us kids not to play "The Jolly Coppersmith" when she knew he would be coming for a visit. I could well understand her concern for the floor, and the minor earthquakes he seemed to cause. Really though, at times the dishes would rattle and the house seemed to shake. Mom was probably afraid her children would take up dancing German style.

Occasionally I hear some of these old tunes played on a TV or radio station, but with a different beat, and I reminisce a little about the old player piano, a machine and a musical instrument that typified an important era of the 20th century. Radio and TV blew it away though, except for the memories, and as these two songs go:

"Memories" and "You Can't Take That Away from Me."

Francis E. Hager
Sun City, Arizona

Memories of the Cookcar

I see our home on the farm around 1925. It is neat and freshly painted white and green. It looks cool but the sun is shining on it. The doors are closed; it looks dark and empty. There are no cooking smells from inside. My mother lives there.

Now, in our yard, right in front of our home about 10 feet to the south, is a monstrous cookcar. Inside are three jolly cooks. My cousin, Helen, and I are almost the same age—about 5 or 6 years old. We enter the cookcar. There is a long aisle and on both sides of the aisle are two long tables—enough room to seat the crew working on our farm, my grandfather's and my uncle's farms, all of which are situated around us. There is a large iron stove in the kitchen in the back.

Helen and I can go in when we are hungry and be served. This day we have hot cinnamon rolls and coffee. We just love the cooks—they are so much fun. And we know they love us. We only can go there when it is empty and the men are not eating. Little girls can't be where men are.

Esther E. Kyllonen Briatico
Bensenville, Illinois

My Most Favorite Day

It happened on a hot summer day when I was 11 years old. Mother was busy canning vegetables from the garden on our black cob wood stove. There was plenty of room on the stove to cook a pot of vegetable soup. Cabbage, carrots, onions and potatoes fresh from the garden were delicious in soup, especially after Mother added fresh, sweet cream just before we ate it.

We had vegetable soup only when Father was not there to eat with us. He didn't care much for vegetables, and vegetable soup was definitely a no-no. It was harvest season and Father and a group of neighbors formed a cooperative threshing crew. Therefore Mother, my younger brother and I could have soup.

This particular day, after the cows were milked, the cream was separated and the eggs were gathered, Mother said, "It's so hot in the house, let's eat outdoors." We had never eaten outdoors. There was no picnic table. Mother brought a chair out for herself, put the soup on a large block, and my brother and I sat on the ground. The soup tasted extra special that day.

After he had finished eating, my brother went off to see how high he could throw clods of dirt. My mother got a brush from the house. She brushed my hair and braided it while we just talked before we washed the dirty dishes.

Money couldn't buy the enjoyment I felt that evening.

Marion Podany
Petersburg, Nebraska

Christmas Dinners and Country Fairs

My folks moved from Chattanooga, Tennessee, to a farm in Soddy Daisy, Tennessee, in 1932 during the Depression era. My grandfather bought the farm to provide us a place to live. The house hadn't been occupied for a year or two when we moved there. The lawn and all surroundings had grown—such sage grass, briars and weeds—it seemed as though we were living in a jungle. We soon cleaned that away, since there were seven people to do the job.

Our neighbor loaned my father a mule and a plow and we started growing corn, peas and hay, plus other garden vegetables to provide us with our livelihood. We all had chores to do to maintain a prosperous farm. Mother processed milk products and sold them. This provided a small added income for us. There was a natural pond on the farm where we sometimes fished when we found the time to do so. We also picked blackberries that grew close to the pond. Mother raised turkeys and Father raised chickens. Mother always prepared a large delicious meal for Thanksgiving and Christmas for the family and any of the relatives who wanted to visit us during the holidays. Father also raised hogs, and we had all the ham we wanted to eat. Preparing the food for winter required quite a bit of work in the summer. Mother canned everything she could to feed us during the winter months.

There is one comical incident that happened on the farm that I will never forget. My two older sisters had to wash the dishes every night after supper. If the one washing dishes got ahead of the one drying the dishes, she would open the kitchen door that led to the back porch and knock on the door three or four times. The sister in the kitchen would sing, "Who's that knocking on my door?" The sister on the porch would answer, "I'm Barnacle Bill the Sailor." (Do you remember that song?) Our father would yell at them, "If you don't get those dishes done, I'm going to knock on your door." He meant he would paddle their backsides with a wooden paddle, and boy that hurt.

We had one reward we looked forward to every year, and that was a trip to the fair in Chattanooga. The day before our planned trip, Dad would say to all of us, "OK kids, if you want to go to the fair tomorrow, you had better pick that field of peas today before I get home from work." We worked so hard to get the job done by the time he arrived home. These memories of our wonderful life on the farm will remain with me as long as I live.

Marvin Stuart
Soddy Daisy, Tennessee

Neighbors and Friends

Neighbors and friends were an important part of rural communities, especially during the years when transportation wasn't as plentiful as it is today. Neighbors were relied upon for assistance in general farming practices, such as making hay, threshing, harvesting corn (especially when it was picked by hand), butchering, driving cattle, etc. Women depended on neighboring women for their social life as well as for assistance and support when serious illness occurred or there were "threshing" dinners to prepare.

My mother served as midwife to many neighboring women, assisting in the delivery of their babies. She seemed to be "on call" and certainly a "beeper" was unheard of then. The neighbor's husband or another neighbor came to request her services when that critical time came to deliver a baby in the home or to assist the doctor if he had arrived.

Farm women led a life of isolation but never wanted for something to do to fill their time. The daily household duties amply used the daylight hours, and when twilight arrived, it was indeed time for rest.

Visiting, cards and games were the entertainment when neighbors did get together for a few hours in the slack seasons. Before radio, telephone and television, you relished each bit of news learned from an afternoon or evening visit.

I recall when my brother contracted polio and was critically ill for weeks, a group of neighbors prepared a big box of wrapped gifts for him—he could open one gift a day for a month. We all benefited from the excitement each day of watching him unwrap the gifts that those neighbors so generously made possible.

In my pre-teen years, my mother made matching dresses for my friend, who was a close neighbor, and me. We delighted in dressing as twins occasionally. Her mother also made us another matching outfit to wear for church and school. We kids spent many long evenings at the Edwards' house playing Monopoly as well as outdoor games.

A means of earning spending money for a young farm girl was

often to work as a "hired girl" for a neighbor who had illness or a new baby in the home. As I was the youngest of three girls, I didn't hire out as often as the older ones did. I recall my oldest sister working for a neighboring family with three boys and earning $1.50 a week. In my late teens I did some working out and baby-sitting—50 cents a night was my earnings for baby-sitting.

I was hired by a neighbor to lead the "hay horse" one summer—I was usually a bit fearful of those big horses trailing so close behind me, but it was a means of earning spending money so I tried very hard to keep a step ahead of the horse. It must've worked since I don't have any scars to show, and the few dollars I earned were cherished.

One Halloween night we kids went to our dear neighbors' house to scare them. The man knew we were coming and put on a sheet and came flying around the corner of the house about the time we were ready to make noises to scare them. We certainly didn't waste any time leaving the scene. He laughed about that for years.

We all are blessed with idiosyncrasies or peculiarities and I recall a few of some neighbors that we still chuckle about today:

One family left their dinner plates on the table at noon when they had finished eating, so they could use the same one that night for supper—it saved washing dishes.

One family filled a big dishpan full with garden lettuce to place under the table, it was convenient for all to help themselves when they wanted some.

One mother, when the child grew tired of chewing his gum, would chew it until the child was ready for it again, and then return it to him. Remember, this was during the Depression so nothing was wasted.

Neighbors and friends are a delightful part of growing up in rural America. Those friendships and good deeds are responsible for many good memories!

Margaret Blair
Lorimor, Iowa

A Busy, Happy Family

Growing up on the family farm lends an influence that lasts a lifetime.

My father was a farm boy, the youngest of three sons. He left home early and became a self-taught barber in the village of Plevna, Missouri. He soon found a young farm girl who became his wife. They built a barber shop of their own in the country village.

With the arrival of their first son, they felt the need for their own home and wanted a bit of land to help make a better life for the family.

At the edge of the village was a small bungalow home on 18 acres of land. They managed to purchase the property and moved to their first farm. Soon they bought a milk cow and a pig; my grandmother added 12 laying hens and a fine rooster to the little farm. Since Grandmother had given these hens to my mother, Mother always claimed the chicken business was hers. She cared for them, gathered the eggs from her flock and sent them to the nearby village store and sold them in exchange for sugar, flour and necessities. Any money that remained after the sale was "Mother's Money." When I was growing up, it always seemed that the egg money met every need of the home.

I, the only daughter in the family, was born in 1916. By that time my dear parents had acquired an additional 40 acres of farming land. My father continued to operate his country barber shop, and with the help of Mother and two sons he took care of the farm.

With the purchase of another acreage and a piece of land acquired by Mother as inheritance, he had a small farm operation working very well. The two brothers helped with the farm work and I assisted our mother.

We were a busy, happy family. In the Missouri springtime, planting season required corn, oats, kafir corn, gardens and potato patches to be planted. We had cows that had to have grain and hay. Father bought a small flock of sheep and we had a work team of horses and a riding horse. Mother's laying hens and young chickens also required grain for feed.

The garden, as well as the poultry, was part of Mother's chores. The garden had to be cared for and the produce canned and preserved. We put out an orchard of apple and peach trees, and within our backyard we had a grouping of Damson plum trees. In our own woods we had walnut and hickory trees from which we harvested nuts for winter use. We also grew a few rows of popcorn in the garden, thus being sure of popcorn and apples for evening food in the long, cold winter evenings.

We had an Edison phonograph that played records that resounded through a large metal horn. We thought this good music. My father bought a piano for my use, and a nearby music teacher gave me lessons.

We subscribed to several good magazines. The *Capper's Weekly* and the weekly *Kansas City Star* were always at our reading table. We read at night by the light from kerosene lamps. The long winter evenings were pleasant as we sat by our wood-burning fire, reading and finding apples and popcorn for family treats. In later years we enjoyed a radio, but it is good to remember those early days when we were happy with books and magazines and the shining clean light of the kerosene lamps. It was a daily chore to keep those lamp flues clean and the bowls filled with kerosene.

One of our acreages was some distance from our home ground. This particular ground boasted a good river on the land. The "Big Fabius River" was filled with catfish and carp. My brothers and Father liked to fish and caught many good-sized ones.

Some of my choice memories recall times when we stayed overnight at this river, set bank-fishing lines and caught nice strings of plentiful catfish. The work seemed like part of a picnic.

Christmastime was a joy at the farm. Our village school always had the program at the local village church. There was a tall tree, beautifully decorated. The whole farming community came to the Christmas program, which honored the Christ child. The countryside was filled with small farms and farm children. The church was always filled to capacity on Christmas evening.

Church and school were always well attended. Old Settlers celebrations and Fourth of July gatherings within our own Knox county were always well attended and were part of the pleasures that came along with growing up on the farm.

We had good neighbors, good friends and a wealth of good memories to carry us through coming years.

Father and Mother gave us a good childhood and a good home, for which I am forever grateful.

Margaret Stout
Plevna, Missouri

The Old Homestead

My maternal grandparents lived on the old homestead about two and a half miles from where we lived. Two of my aunts and an uncle still lived with them. When my parents went to town shopping, my three older brothers and I would stay with them.

I can remember one Saturday afternoon when I was about 4 years old, I wanted to go to town with my parents instead of staying with my grandparents. I started to cry and make a fuss. Grandma reached into the pocket of her black-and-white checked apron and gave me a pink peppermint candy. It soothed my hurt feelings.

The kitchen was the center of activity. I remember the tan-and-green cookstove that burned wood and cobs. There was a long table in the center that could seat 10 people. A cupboard with glass doors on the top part sat in a corner. I could see the pretty dishes in there. An open shelf in the middle held a tin box of buttons, mending supplies and the latest papers and periodicals. There was a bucket with a dipper in it that sat on a bench by the window that held drinking water. The water was very hard, as the inside of the bucket was coated with lime.

The pantry off the kitchen interested me the most. There were shelves on one side and a table in the corner. A coffee grinder was fastened to the wall by the door. Aunt Martha let me turn the handle on the coffee grinder to make coffee for supper. I really felt I was a big girl when I could do that. There was a big crock jar covered with a dishtowel that held cookies. Gingersnaps were my favorite. On the table was a long, store-bought summer sausage. Aunt Martha cut slices of homemade bread from the loaf in the bread box to make sandwiches with the sausage. With some of the cookies, this was afternoon lunch for my brothers and me. The summer sausage was a real treat for us, as we did not have that kind of meat at home.

To keep me entertained Aunt Amie gave me some thread and a needle to string buttons. I would go through the tin box and pick out the prettiest ones. When I had several buttons on the thread I wore it as a necklace. This was the first thing that I showed my mother when they returned from town.

Later in life I had a button collection, and I still like pink peppermint candy.

Vida Sunderman
Norfolk, Nebraska

Barns Helped Make Childhoods Happy

I could never imagine growing up anywhere except on a farm. The food we had was different from what we enjoy today. The radio took us into the imaginary roles that we played depending on the hour of the day or day of the week. The barn was a castle that I could reign in and in my mind close out all the problems of the world.

Most of our meals were happy times for sharing. Our main meal through the weekdays was breakfast. If we were to have meat, such as chicken, ham, pork chops or any other meat dish, we usually had it in the morning. If we caught a chicken from the yard to eat we would put it up for a few days prior to killing it. I suppose it was to feed it clean grain so it would be clean to eat. At one time we had put a chicken under a cotton basket to feed. Imagine my dad's surprise when he reached under the basket expecting to find two chicken legs but instead he caught hold of two cat legs that were scratching him. The problem began when my younger brother was playing with the chicken and it got away. He couldn't catch the chicken, but the cat was close by so he made the switch.

The radio was a very important part of our lives. We would look forward to hearing Henry Aldridge saying, "Coming Mother," or Lum answering the phone, "Jottom down store Lum speaking." Baby Snooks was always welcome in our home. One afternoon I stopped at my grandmother's, who lived next to us. She was crying. I asked her what the problem was and she informed me that Jack Armstrong, the all-American Boy, had been forced to kill someone. He had never killed before. The next day the victim proved to be well on his way to recovery and all was well.

I don't understand how anyone could ever have a happy childhood without a barn. Ours was used for storing hay, peanuts and all kinds of goods. The stock was housed downstairs, but the loose hay was stored up in the loft. The loft was my domain on a rainy or otherwise dreary day. Even now, after more than 50 years have passed, I can see a barn and it brings back so many happy memories of my childhood. I could lay up on the loose hay and plan the future. I could dive or jump from the upper rafters and imagine I was leaping from my flaming bomber or springing from a high diving board. I loved the quiet time that old barn brought. I wish every person could have one in their past.

Looking back on these important parts of my past makes the hard times seem more like happy times and helps to bury them away forever. Even though these times took place some 50 or 60 years ago they seem like only last week.

Clyde J. Posey
Cleveland, Alabama

———■———

Chapter 9: Time-Honored Traditions

Captains of the Cornstalk Boats

Spending a Sunday at Grandmother and Grandfather's large house with a spacious porch was memorable. After a long church service, my brothers and sister and nearby cousins, all of us dressed in our Sunday best, flocked to the table along with the grownups. Sometimes an extra table would have to be set to accommodate the brood.

There was chicken and dumplings, mashed potatoes, yams, green beans and platters of corn from the field. And always, there was Grandmother's fruit cake. Made with sorghum molasses, it consisted of eight to 10 thin layers held together, then covered with a brown paste made of evaporated apples from their orchard and flavored with various spices.

After dinner my grandparents and the elders sat on the long porch watching the bees droning over the vast clover field. Finally, Grandmother would don her crisp bonnet that matched her Sunday apron, Grandfather would loosen his tie and adjust his gold watch fob and hand in hand they would stroll through the fields of growing and ripening vegetables. Often Grandmother came in with cucumbers or cantaloupes snuggled in the folds of her apron.

After borrowing paring knives and scissors from the kitchen, the children headed for the cornfield to gather old stalks, which they cut, slit and made into boats and rafts in the shade of the apple tree. Ah, the age of innocence and of inventiveness.

When our ships were ready, we raced barefoot down to the waterway that trickled around the skirt of the hill. The hill rose up from the edge of the water. At some points there were cliffs hanging out over the water, where small wrens nested. Once the boat captains set their crafts afloat, they followed along the stream with long sticks to dislodge their boats from rocks or debris. Along the voyage the children paused to peer inside wrens' nests at blue speckled eggs or naked baby birds with closed eyes and open mouths. Farther and farther downstream the older children guided their fleet, while the younger ones paused to catch polliwogs and put them in jars of water.

These activities continued until the sun set over the western hills and deep shadows darkened the water. Then the boats were anchored in the reeds.

Grandmother's voice sent us scampering back to the house, where we indulged in another meal. This time it was leftovers and hot biscuits with honey or jam, take your choice, and tall glasses of milk. Several of the young boat captains are no longer with us, but how treasured are their memory.

Edna Densford
Carlsbad, California

Family Dinners

I remember the large family dinners we had when I was a small boy. The women and girls of the family would put the food on a long table in the shade of the yard. One or two of the younger girls would wave green leafy branches over the table to keep the flies away.

At one of these family dinners when I was a little boy, I had a nice chicken drumstick, my favorite piece because it had such a good handle. My mother took it from me, took all of the meat off of it, then gave the bone to one of my little cousins so he could chew on it. I was so disappointed! She had ruined my drumstick, and I never did like that child after that.

Kenneth Crouch
Trenton, Missouri

The Typical Farmer

The average farmer rose at about five o'clock in the morning and went to the barn to milk his cows. He was quiet and gentle with them and even squirted warm milk into the cats' mouths. One by one he let the cows out.

The large containers of milk were carried to the separator house. The handle on the separator was rotated until the little bell quit ringing and the milk was run through the machine. The cream ran into a separate receptacle and the skim milk was fed to the pigs.

As the farmer carried the skim milk to the hog house, every pig made a ruckus, begging to be fed.

By this time, the roosters were crowing and the hens were chirping. The cream check from the dairy herd and the daily egg gathering took care of the weekly household expenses.

Breakfast was next. The menu varied according to how laborious the day was to be. If it was field work, haying or picking corn, the meal could consist of bacon, ham and eggs, toast, jelly and coffee. Sometimes cereal and fried potatoes were added. After breakfast the farmer finished his chores, harnessed his horses and headed for the fields.

The mowers, rakes and hayracks were used in force during haying time. Corn planters were pulled by horses as were the binders when the grain was ready to be harvested. Barns were cleaned and manure spreaders fertilized the fields. There were no idle moments, but when the farm couple caught up with their tasks, they would go to town to do any business they needed to do and spend the rest of the day visiting.

If a neighbor was ill or had undergone surgery, the rest of the neighbors would pitch in and take care of his crop. The wives would go along with baskets of food to feed the hungry workers. Wasn't that great?

When winter came, the sled was used to haul wood or possibly to take the children to meet the school bus. If the country road was blocked, all of the farmers would come, armed with shovels, to help open the road.

Probably one of the most important jobs for the children was to keep the wood boxes filled and the reservoirs filled with water, so hot water was always available.

People visited each other, sometimes to play cards or have house dances. There was a real community spirit that people would never forget.

Madonna L. Storla
Postville, Iowa

Grandpa's Farm was Paradise

A trip on the train with Mom and three younger brothers was an event in my young life, because we were always on our way to Grandpa's.

Grandpa's 60 acres of rolling hills—with its bubbling spring, the swing under the huge old elm, the sand pile under the row of maples, the colony of bees in the new orchard, the persimmon tree and the "branch" running at the foot of the hill on which the new house stood—was paradise to the four of us. We waded in the runoff from the spring, caught fat frogs and toads, played house with big acorn cups under the enormous oak by the road, followed the cow paths through the pasture, squeezed between the rails of the pasture fence, and waded in the shallow sand-bedded "branch" on warm summer days.

Sometimes Mom would leave me there for a week, probably more for her own vacation than for mine. Then I played in the pasture with the little lambs, nestled in the corners of the rail fence making clover chains, caught the little gray lizards under the concrete bridge, or maybe turned the huge grindstone while Grandpa sharpened his scythe or Grandma's hoe.

These lovely vacations were not entirely free rides. My duties included keeping the wood box full for Grandma and bringing buckets of water from the well with its long, bottom-valved bucket hung on a pulley from the top of a tripod of rails. It was my job to gather the eggs laid by the multi-colored hens and to help

Grandma shell corn into her apron to feed them. I set the table and dried dishes. I also ate fresh, buttered light bread with gobs of honey. I carried Grandma's wondrous sugar cookies about with me while playing. It was a pleasure to carry Grandpa's water jug and a sack of cookies to the field where he was plowing.

We would sit in the shade of a persimmon tree while he and his team rested from the walking plow, his cane hanging on the cross bar. Then we talked, for he was deaf, and I refused to talk to him when anyone else was around. He told me about the tadpoles in the little pond where the wagon or the buggy sat to soak the loosened felloes. He told me about the bugs we saw and named the grasses and weeds around us, the wild blossoms, even the birds that followed his plow when I wasn't back there scaring them away. When he walked the gullied slope on the far side of the run with the grass seeder over his shoulder, my job was to carry his cane until he tired. Then we'd sit and he'd tell me about the different trees and bushes—the elderberry and poke, the slim paw-paws at the crest of the hill and the walnut and hickory in the little stand of timber over yonder.

When blackberries and dewberries were ripe, Mom would bring us to the farm and we would pick berries among the briar patches and the chiggers. Chiggers were a commonplace cause of itching and scratching.

Summer nights on the farm were spent on the front porch, listening to katydids and whippoorwills, to Grandma and Grandpa talking. Winter nights were pleasant by the wood stove, Grandma knitting new heels into his gray wool socks, he reading his farming magazines, including *Capper's*.

There are oceans of memories attached to that old clay hill farm in Wayne County, Illinois, including that of a courageous, polio-crippled ex-teacher trying too late in life to bring back to productivity a washed-out piece of land, the strength of his wife and helpmate and the marvelous resourcefulness of both.

Myrtle Pierson
Monticello, Illinois

Fun-Filled Christmases of the Past

On the farm, our Christmas tree was always a pasture ever-green put in a five-gallon bucket filled with sand or rocks to hold it upright. Our decorations were quite simple, but we thought they were beautiful—strung popcorn, chains of paper, either construction paper cut in strips or colored with Crayolas, a few treasured glass balls (wish I still had them), and of course, icicles. I can remember having clip-on candle holders with candles but can never remember lighting the candles. Mother probably realized what a fire hazard they would be. We hung wreaths in the windows and "honeycomb" bells in the doorways. Our tree was always in the parlor, since we didn't heat that room, so we placed it near the see-through "French doors" in order to enjoy it.

Breakfast and outdoor farm chores were done before we were allowed to open any presents. Our presents were quite simple—mostly clothes that we really needed, maybe a doll or homemade doll clothes, books or games. We had an orange and some hard candy in our socks. There were gifts from the grandparents too, nothing elaborate by today's standards to be sure, but we were always proud and appreciative of whatever we received.

Christmas dinner was always special. I never remember having turkey, usually pork or roast beef or maybe roast chicken and dressing, fluffy mashed potatoes, hot homemade rolls with lots of butter and jelly, home-canned green beans or scalloped corn with oysters, gelatin salads and pumpkin or mincemeat pie after dinner. We stuffed ourselves with homemade candy, fudge, divinity and peanut brittle. After a fun-filled day with various grandparents, uncles, aunts and cousins, it was time to bundle up and do the evening chores: feed the chickens and the hogs, gather the eggs and milk the cows. After that another Christmas was tucked away in our memory.

Ann Wyer
Corydon, Iowa

Church in the Country

We lived way out in the country and there was no church in our area. We had permission to meet for Sunday School in the one-room schoolhouse about a half-mile from our home. The Sunday School was under the direction of the Scandinavian Baptist Conference, but they seldom had a minister come for preaching service. A.K. Tollefson, a man who was a farmer and a preacher, often came to conduct a worship service.

In the schoolhouse we had a small square Victrola and a few records for music appreciation class. One record I recall was, "Oh, It's Nice To Get Up In The Morning But It's Nicer to Lie In Bed." When Mr. Tollefson, who was a fairly large man, came to preach, he would set the Victrola on the corner of the teacher's desk for his pulpit. The Victrola had no cover but he could lay his Bible and notes on the turntable. Often when he wished to emphasize a point he would slap his hand down sharply on his notes. He did this often. Much later at school when we put records on the Victrola to play, the teacher noticed that the turntable slanted to one side, but we children never told her what had caused it.

In the mid 1920s, my father, John Hoien, bought a two-pole circus tent and set it up by our corncrib. He wrote to a minister to come and hold meetings for our community. These meetings lasted for several weeks. We had hoped that a church would be organized but that didn't happen. Then in the late 1920s, my grandfather, Soren C. Anderson, decided to do something about it. He hired contractors and had a church built on some of his property. He paid for the entire building, but family and neighbors paid for the pews, piano and pulpit. This church served the community for many, many years. After automobiles became common and people were willing to drive farther to church the building was unused for a time. Then a group bought it and moved it to Aberdeen for their use.

Eunice Hoien Dahlgren
Sweet Home, Oregon

Our Musical Family

Our family was a musical one. Dad was a natural fiddle player and Mama read music and could play for hours too—without the notes. We five kids all sang and harmonized 'round the piano. Often times neighbors would call and want to hear our folks play, and they would listen on the old-time telephone. They would visit us too and join in the music. We kids were all in music at school, as well as the big plays.

Mother would walk up to the church house before Christmas to teach the musical parts of a cantata to the children. Other ladies would help with the speaking parts.

The tree would be a huge one that touched the high ceiling. Its ornaments wouldn't be fancy. Gifts were simple, such as 10-cent silk hankies, 5-cent cotton ones, beads, color books and crayons, combs, brushes, necklaces, books and other items that cost a fraction of what they would now.

A big plump Santa Claus always thrilled us all with his bag of oranges and candy. He came in with a big, "Ho, Ho, Ho."

We kids still believed in Santa until a girl from the city told us it was our parents. I remember how the little girls cried.

The school Christmas program was a delight. We practiced it over and over again so it would be good for all the parents to see. As at church, we drew names and always bought our teacher a gift too. The only money we had for buying gifts was from picking up, hulling and drying the black walnuts on our hillside. Our hands would really be stained—but how proud each of us would be with our 85 or 90 cents to buy gifts for the names we drew, our teacher, parents, and our brothers and sisters.

It was usually a bad day when we went to Christmas shop. Dad would load up our walnuts in the wagon. Mama would heat bricks so our feet would keep partially warm under the heavy quilt. After we got our precious little coins, off to the dime store we went to buy our gifts. We were cautious not to spend all of our cash before each gift was bought.

Mama would take the five of us to Heer's basement, where she treated us each to a delicious bowl of vegetable soup and crackers. My, I think I can still see those bowls of 5-cent soup. Yum, yum.

The ride home was chilly—but we were happy with the small pleasures in life.

Ruth Marie McMillan
Buffalo, Missouri

A Lifetime of Wild Flowers

My story begins in the 1930s when I was going to a country school for the first years of my education. The school was a little over a mile from our house. The only road to get there could hardly be called a road. It was more like a grass path, and I can't remember a snow plow opening it in the winter.

Today all the controversy over half-day or all-day kindergarten seems ridiculous to me. We had kindergarten and first grade all in one year and thought nothing of it. This allowed me to graduate from high school at 16 and immediately move into helping make a farming operation a success. My wife and I are still on the same farm, which has now been in the family for well over 100 years.

The old country school is long gone, but the memories of it are still very much alive. Since it was easier to walk across the fields than to go on the old road, this is what my brother and I did, every day, no matter how deep the snow.

These walks were a perfect opportunity for a small boy to pick wild flowers on land that was not farmed at that time. I soon found I pleased my parents by doing this, so I did it often. Later I pleased my wife by taking time to pick flowers for her too. My grandchildren enjoy getting in on the act nowadays. My parents have been gone physically for some time, but their boy still takes flowers from the fields and garden to their graves many times a year, even up until the snow flies. As long as the good Lord is willing, I am going to continue for my wife and the memory of my parents.

Virgil Denner
New Hampton, Iowa

Stoves: A Family Gathering Place

My childhood remembrances include the stoves with their nurturing warmth. Our old house had a baseburner. On cold mornings we would bring our clothes and dress around its comforting potbelly with the isinglass reflecting vigorous flames. As a 5-year-old I remember the midwife holding our new baby sister there on a November evening.

In the new house a basement furnace circulated heat to the upper floors, though I don't remember the upstairs bedrooms being heated. I read a poem once in which the poet gave tribute to her father's early rising to start the fire so there was warmth when the family arose. This unsung task Dad did before he went out to milk and do chores.

Adjacent to the furnace was a coal bin or room with an outside metal opening in which coal deliverers would hoist the coal. Wood was also burned. We had three huge cottonwood trees at the edge of the grove, so huge that it took several of us holding hands to reach around them. One year Dad felt he had to sacrifice one of them for wood. It was a jolt I can still remember.

In the center of the kitchen was the cookstove, with its commodious top accommodating high heat on the front or warming toward the back. There was the reservoir, which warmed rain water for washing dishes. Above were warming ovens, where among other things Mom dried eggshells, which she then crushed and gave to the hens as a calcium supplement. As a child I remember loving to go and stand in the cubby space behind the stove, a place of warmth and privacy for a little girl.

In time we added an oil stove, a white enamel contraption on spindly legs that had three burners and an oven on the left. In the summer this was a welcome option to heating up the cookstove.

My aunt had a small cylindrical oil heater that added area heat. In later days it was an antique object on which she placed a plant.

At our country one-room school a huge stove surrounded by a circular metal shield filled the back part of the room. The teacher, who earned $25 a month, had the duty of getting there early to start the stove and keep it fed during the day. There was a flat surface on top, where at noon we heated hot dishes that our mothers took turns sending. My mom made a macaroni dish in tomato sauce that I dearly loved.

My first experience with an electric stove was graphic. We visited my modern cousin Edith in town, and in inspecting her new stove I naively put my hand on the burner and experienced a quick withdrawal.

My husband tells of his dad heating bricks, wrapping them and putting them in bed by the children's feet at night. We used flannel sheets and huddled under mounds of homemade quilts. The windows had beautiful Jack Frost sculptures through which we peered on a winter wonderland, beautiful yet harsh as one ventured out to do chores or navigated to school, town or church. If one has warmth and nurturing within, one can weather the storms without.

Bernice Severson
Portland, Oregon

"Yule Buk" Fun Time

At Christmas time in our predominately Norwegian neighborhood, people celebrated for a whole week. Farmers went visiting after their chores were done or entertained in their own homes.

"Yule Buk" was Norwegian for Christmas Fooling. It was a lot of fun. People dressed in comical costumes and wore masks. They usually walked from one farm to the other to see if their identity could be guessed. The ridiculous clothing they wore and the fact that they disguised their voices made this difficult.

Householders guessed many times and often the "foolers" got away without being guessed correctly.

At most places they were invited in for wine or coffee and cookies—but only if someone guessed who they were.

One evening, the neighborhood men gathered at one house to play cards in honor of the first born. The wives cleverly decided to be Yule Buks. The men were thoroughly surprised, and most of the women escaped without being identified.

Somehow, this clever little game has fallen by the wayside. It was a lot of fun, but the younger generation want to get in their cars and do something new and different.

Madonna L. Storla
Postville, Iowa

Snow Days and Saturday Baths

When I was growing up, Saturday night was time for a bath, but you didn't just turn on the faucet. Water was pumped and carried in from the well and heated, either in the reservoir on the back of the cookstove or on the heating stove. Cobs—often picked up after the hogs had eaten the corn off—wood or coal were burned in the stove, and all had to be carried in. Water was put in a round galvanized tub beside the stove. Once my brother got too close and burned his backside. I wonder if he still has a scar.

Our cookstove oven had other uses than baking. My dad often warmed his feet on the open door. Many mornings I would wake up to the baa of a lamb, the squeal of little pigs or the peep of baby chicks, all of which needed to be warmed to survive. Occasionally a new calf might need to be warmed up too.

There were no snow days at our school. Since we lived some distance away, when the roads were blocked with snow, Dad hitched Bonnie and Bell—our team of black horses—to the bobsled and put lots of straw in it. Mother heated a soapstone to keep our feet warm and wrapped us in a horsehide robe. Dad donned his heavy sheepskin coat and heavy mittens and we were off over the drifts. We never missed a day.

Marie Denner
New Hampton, Iowa

Chapter 10: Visits to Remember

The Scary Attic

When I was a child, my parents would take us to spend a week with our grandparents who lived about 100 miles away. Their home was a very large farmhouse without modern conveniences. We enjoyed our visits there. Grandpa always made us oatmeal for breakfast, but he would start it before he went to bed. He would fill a double boiler with the necessary ingredients and place it on the back of the old wood stove, where it cooked slowly all night. In the morning Grandma would make the most delicious little oval-shaped muffins to go with the oatmeal. We never forgot those wonderful preserves that Grandma and Grandpa worked together to make. Our mother used to try to copy that simple breakfast, but it never was as good as it was at Grandpa's house.

Grandpa had several cows, a horse, a few pigs and chickens. He grew tame berries of all kinds. We would eat them to our hearts' content. Mom was always afraid we would eat too many and get sick, but we never did. We'd hunt for the little harmless grass snakes that hid in the stone fence along the dirt road, then we'd run like crazy if we saw one.

It was so much fun until bedtime. Grandma and Mother would walk with the lamp ahead of us to the third floor, which was the attic. It was filled with the usual things. There was a bed with a feather mattress that was only used when we came to visit. My sister and I always had to sleep there. After they heard our prayers and tucked us in, they'd leave, taking the lamp with them. If we were lucky, the moon would shine through a very small window. We'd lay there in the dark thinking all sorts of scary things. One night I was awakened by someone trying to pull the blankets off of me. I yelled to my sister to wake up. She was awake. We both started screaming. Dad and Mom came running in with a candle.

"What's going on in here?" Dad wanted to know.

"Someone is pulling the blankets off of us," I cried. Our parents started to laugh, and told us to sit up. We did and found that we were facing each other. Somehow I had gotten to the bottom of the bed. The harder I'd pull, the harder she'd pull. We almost succeeded in scaring each other to death.

Helen Caron
Massena, New York

Fun at Grandpa and Grandma's

I like to go to my grandpa and grandma's farm. It's fun to help with the chores, see the new baby calves and help move the cows from one field to another. It is fun to just watch all the animals and to be out with Grandpa when he's getting the crops in out of the fields. I like to ride in the combine and watch the corn and beans come out of the augers into the trucks.

My grandma has a garden, and I help her pick vegetables from it when they are ready. I like the pumpkins best, because Grandma lets me take some home and make jack-o'-lanterns from them.

There is an old railroad bed near the house. My cousins, my sister and I like to walk on the path because we can find many neat rocks, some old railroad spikes and many little things we can take home and show to Grandma.

I ride the four-wheeler with my dad and we sometimes go to the timber and have a picnic and a wiener roast when the wind isn't blowing too hard.

Sara Ann Wyer
Corydon, Iowa

A City Girl in the Country

In 1944, when my husband, Randy, and I were married, money was scarce except for what we needed for life's necessities. Randy's cousin, Cecil, had a 320-acre farm in Roanoke, Virginia, and he invited us to come visit him and his wife, Evelyn, on our honeymoon. My husband was born in Roanoke, but I was born in New York City. It was dark when we arrived at the farm and Randy made a sudden sharp turn off the narrow mountain road. I thought he had fallen asleep so I screamed before I realized he was only turning onto Cecil's property.

Cecil and Evelyn were waiting for us, and it was at this little farmhouse that I learned the meaning of southern hospitality. They were about 10 years older than we were but had not as yet been blessed with children. Soon after we had our first boy, they had their first girl. We had three more boys in the years to come and Cecil and Evelyn had another daughter and a son.

Going back to our first visit, here was a city gal on a real farm with cows, horses, pigs, chickens, etc. The farmhouse had no bathroom and the outhouse was about a football field away. Naturally I had to pay "jon" a visit in the middle of the night—so with Randy and a flashlight in tow, we dodged cow patties all the way.

Now you might think that from this first experience, a city girl would want no part of a farm ever again, but I learned a lot about picking berries, canning, making jam, cooking side meat with green beans, cleaning and cooking southern fried chicken, etc. For two weeks I became a real live country girl and loved every minute of it. Our children learned to fish and hunt and take long treks in the woods. They learned to skin squirrels and rabbits that Evelyn would cook up with red-eye gravy and biscuits. Mmm mmm that was good eatin'.

For 15 years we spent our summer vacations at Cecil and Evelyn's, and while Cecil is no longer with us, we still go back to the farm to visit Evelyn, who's 82 now.

Gloria Agee
Walnut Cove, North Carolina

The Work Got Done While We Were Having Fun

When I was a child and would visit Grandpa and Grandma on their farm, we'd have fun, but I noticed that while we were having fun, the work they had to do got done. We would pick green beans, gather pears, or hunt the cows that had calves.

Times don't change very much. Our granddaughter, whose teacher teaches phonics and urges creativity instead of spelling, wrote the following story for her second-grade English assignment:

"Yestur day I stad with grampa and gramma on their farm. They said they had work to do but I could help.

"I helpd them burn a naro strip of ded grass around ther garden. The cat and us checkd the big bales of hay for mise. We plantd flower bubbs and unyun sets. We cleand grammas utilaty room and grampas tak shed. Grampa has lots of sadles, sadle blankets, bridles, halters, and even spurs. We tore down ther old bruder house bekase they don't raise chickens any more. We walkd to the spring at the back side of thar place and cleand the sand and junk out of it so it'd run clean. We pickd up cans and trash that drivrs had throne out on the rode. We made yest bred and I got to help need the dow, but gramma made me wash my hands real good first.

Gramma used her pinking shears and cut me a bandana from materiel I chose out of her scrap box. She told me about when daddy was a boy and what he ust to do. We fed the horse and all the caves. Gramma calls them baby darlins. We cookd grampa ham and beens for dinner and we had winter unyuns out of his garden and the bread I helpd make. It was a good dinner and I helpd fix it. We checkd out grampas trees in the orcherd. Grampa will have pears, apples, cheries, and peachs this summer. We pulld grass in grammas irus beds and she let me take one home to plant. I like to go to grampa and grammas howse."

And the cycle goes on, each generation teaching the next how to find fun in working, enjoying each other and still getting done what needs doing.

Marjorie Buchanan
Pawnee, Oklahoma

Memories for a New Generation

I was born in 1936 in a small Nebraska town of 2000 people. My mother, father and I would visit Aunt Hazel and Uncle Clay's farm, which was four miles from town. We did not always own a car, so we could take the early morning bus that made regular daily runs to Columbus 40 miles away. The driver would let us out at Uncle Clay's lane and we would then walk the half-mile to their house.

Perhaps we would help them can corn, butcher a hog or just spend a day of visiting. We would have a huge delicious meal at noon—usually fried chicken or canned pork, mashed potatoes and gravy and chocolate pie. In the afternoon Aunt Hazel would say, "Play us a tune on the piano, Shirley, while we cool off a bit." Early in the evening, we would walk back up the half-mile lane to the highway, and the bus would pick us up on its return trip.

On one of our summer visiting days, a black cloud came up. Uncle Clay came running to the house and said we should all go to the cave. It was a deep cave. Aunt Hazel, a Baptist teetotaler, said the former owner was a drunkard who had started digging the cave by hand when he was "under the influence." The cave was 27 steps down—a tremendous job to have been done by hand. It was so cool that Aunt Hazel kept her butter, eggs and milk down there. She and Uncle Clay were both tall, slender people, and I think they kept trim by "jazzercizing" up and down those cave steps several times a day.

They did not have electricity and used oil lamps. But one time when we visited them, they had just acquired a new gas light. Aunt Hazel showed it to us but said we would have to wait until Uncle Clay came in to light it as it was very dangerous. It did make quite a hissing sound when lit.

I have so many fond memories of that family farm. I am now a farmer's wife of 38 years, and nieces and nephews from the city visit us. I hope we are providing them with cherished memories too.

Shirley Meis
Elgin, Nebraska

A Weekend at Grandma's House

The wind blew. Thunder and lightning seemed to be at war with each other. Lightning shot, then thunder returned the volley with double force. The sky was dark like a piece of black velvet. Trees bent to the wind, which whistled around corners. Deedee, my little granddaughter, lay curled in my lap trying to be brave. She was ready for bed but the war outside would not let her rest. I sat rocking her as she snuggled in the big rose-green afghan my grandma had made for me many, many years ago. Deedee loved to be bundled up in it. She would say, "I'm all cozy, like a bug in a rug, aren't I Grandma?" I would squeeze her and say, "Yes, Deedee, my little rug bug." Deedee started to say, "Grandma, did..." when a great clap of thunder boomed. She jumped nervously. When the thunder subsided she went on, "Grandma, did you ever visit your grandma?"

"Oh, yes, Deedee, lots of times."

"Will you tell me a story about your grandma, please?"

"Surely. Let's see now... It was Friday night and the beginning of a long weekend in early summer. Your great-grandma and grandpa drove with your Aunt Connie and me down to my grand-ma's house in the little village of Como, which was located just west of Sterling and Rock Falls, Illinois. I knew we were close to Grandma's house because there was a sign in front of a little gray house that said 'FRESH HONEY.' We turned at the corner just beyond that sign, and five minutes down that road was Grandma's house. The gate was open and the yard seemed filled with cars. There was Grandpa's black Ford with yellow spoke wheels, Uncle George's gray coupe, and Uncle Wilbur's maroon Packard that was like a minibus you see today.

"Aunt Dee and my cousin Dean were playing nearby. Aunt Dee was 1 year old, and I was 4 years old. Aunt Laura, my teen-aged aunt, was at the old pump filling a bucket of cold water. Grandma heard us. She came to the front door to welcome us. The sun was just setting as we hurriedly emptied the car and ran to play with our cousins Mavis and Pat. The men went to smoke by the old swing under the big oak tree. The women went into the house to have coffee, and the men had cold beer from cans. We six children chased fireflies. Then it started to sprinkle. Everyone moved indoors. Quickly the house was crowded. Grandma had only three small rooms with lots of large furniture in this house. In the kitchen there was an old stove, a Hoosier cabinet, and a small table with four small chairs. The tiny living room held a big upright piano and a bookcase desk. Grandpa's overstuffed arm-chair sat in the middle of the room, and a six-foot overstuffed sofa-bed was placed along one wall. A 'daybed' stood behind the front door. Grandma's bedroom held two big old dressers, a big baby crib, and a double bed. We squeezed into the house, 15 of us and a few cats and dogs. We had popcorn with lots of homemade butter and tall cold glasses of root beer."

"Where was the bathroom, Grandma?"

"Well, Deedee, it was way down a path out in back. It was called the outhouse or 'privie.' Grandma did not have any flush toilets like we do today.

"Soon beds were prepared. The couch was opened and mat-tresses were flopped on the floor. Blankets and pillows came from somewhere. The rain fell gently when we went to bed. About 1 a.m. the wind started to blow. The thunder and lightning wors-ened, like it has tonight. The river nearby was rising rapidly and began to sound angry. Grandma, hearing the storm, got up to close her windows. This is when I had the scariest experience of my life. Grandma's house had no electric lights, so she lit a kerosene lamp. Just as she reached the kitchen doorway with her lamp a big thun-der clap shook the house. I woke to the sound, and the lightning shone into my eyes. I opened them to see a person in a long white gown with long golden hair streaming down both sides of her shoulders, and she was holding a bright lamp. It was so bright I could not see beyond the lamplight to see her face. I believed that God had sent his angel to collect me and carry me back to heaven. I screamed and screamed. I was so scared. Grandma finally got me quieted after waking up the whole houseful of sleepers."

"Where were you sleeping, Grandma?" Deedee asked.

"I was on the big mattress on the floor with my mother, father, and sister. It scared me when I looked up and saw that bright light and what I thought was an angel.

"In the morning when we woke, the sun was warm and the sky held a few soft clouds drifting lazily along on their carpet of blue. Birds were singing and the flowers smelled sweet. It was a pretty day. After breakfast we took turns driving the old bodiless truck Gramps had in the backyard. We had to sit on a box on the chassis. No seats, no nothing, just four wheels and a box, but it was fun to speed down imaginary roads to see all the wonders of the world. After our turn with the truck we wandered off to play with the new little puppies and with Snowball, the big white cat. Grandpa took us to see Fibber and Molly, the new calves, and to scratch the big white pigs on their long pink snouts. Later we helped Grandma pick strawberries. At least we thought we were helping her, although we were more in the way then not.

"For lunch we had sandwiches and large glasses of fresh milk from Grandpa's Jersey cow. At the supper table, we ate in shifts. First, the kids sat down at the table. We would have pork chops, mashed potatoes and 'hillbilly' gravy, beans, and milk and cookies for dessert. When we finished we went into the yard and the men ate next. After they finished, they went back to the swing and their pipes. The women ate last. Then they did the dishes. They pumped large buckets of water, heated them on the old cookstove, then poured them into a big dishpan on one end of the table. As the dishes were washed they were put into another large dishpan. Hot water was poured over them, then they were dried and put away for another day.

"My aunt put the little ones in the crib for the night, then she and the older children walked down the road to see some pretty flowers in the garden and went to the river to watch the sunset. We lay in the grass, and I looked for the Big and Little Dippers as the crickets chirped and a dog barked somewhere in the distance. We did not want to give up the day that had been so much fun.

"Sunday came, and at noon the ladies would carry out big bowls of food, placing them on a make-shift table, which was actually a sawhorse and an old door. This was covered with a large, white bed-sheet. There were platters of fried chicken, scrapple, corn, baked beans, mounds of mashed potatoes, fresh garden tomatoes and rich milk gravy. Nothing tasted as good as chicken milk gravy. For dessert there were pies and cakes. With our plates piled high we would go to our favorite corner of the yard and eat, returning for seconds and thirds. The men would read the funnies to us from the Sunday paper: Dick Tracy, Orphan Annie, Toots and Casper and other favorites. At midafternoon Grandpa took some of the older children in the old Ford to the local store for ice cream. About 5 o'clock in the evening Grandma made cold meat and cheese sand-wiches for supper, and then we started back home.

"Grandma and Grandpa were plain and simple folks who were so nice to remember. I still smell the honeysuckle, lilacs, and the new-mown hay.

"I wish, Deedee, that I had a place like that for you to visit."

Looking down, I smiled. Deedee had fallen asleep. The moon was shining in the window. All was right with the world, and the world was all right.

Crescence Stadeble
DeKalb, Illinois

The Peaceful Countryside

Born in 1930 on a farm in eastern Kansas, I loved to spend time at my grandparents' home three miles north—beautifully nestled below "Crowell Hill." Egg sales from their hens were their livelihood.

I always slept in an upstairs room. At that certain time of year the aroma of the incubators permeated the "west room" near the walk-in attic, which had a secret drawer that fascinated me so.

Once hatched the baby chicks were placed in their brooder-house around a brick oven. What a delightful sight to see them chirping—so happy—in their new home.

Further west was the henhouse with the straw roof. Hens were disappearing due to a opossum. Knowing that if the hens were gone there would be no money for groceries, my grandmother fixed a bed on a cot and slept in the henhouse. She was able to kill Mr. Opossum when he showed up that night for a big fat hen.

Now living in a large city, I haven't forgotten the peacefulness of being gently awakened each morning by the distant crow of a rooster.

Barbara Foster
Lakewood, Colorado

A Visit to the Farm, Circa 1901

My father describes a visit to the farm of his mother's cousin, Admiral Hiram Paulding, at the turn of the century.

"It was about noon. Up the steep, unpaved country road Kitty Mare and Old Daisy trudged, pulling behind them the surrey and its four occupants. Cousin Hiram was driving and I, a boy of 8, sat beside him. My sister Louise, not yet 6, was in the back with Cousin Virginia. This was my first ride in such a carriage and the excitement gave me a warm feeling inside. Being so close to the horses, I pretended I was at the reins. Their steady trot over the smooth road from the railroad station had been fascinating, and now the slow walk up the hill made me impatient to be moving at a faster pace.

"A heavy rain had begun to fall. As Cousin Hiram urged the team ahead, he said aloud, 'We can put up the curtains when we get to the top of the hill.' Then, as though sensing my unspoken question as to why we must go on in the rain, he turned to me and said, 'The horses can't stop in the middle of a steep hill unless there is a "thank-you-ma'am" on it.'

"I later learned that a thank-you-ma'am was an indentation in the road, like a wide step, which provided a flat surface on which a carriage could rest and not slide back down the hill when the horses stopped pulling.

"The thunder and lightning and rain continued. At the top of the hill we stopped, and Cousin Hiram unrolled the leather curtains with their isinglass windows and snapped each into its position on the sides of the surrey. All secured, we continued on to the farm.

"This was my first prolonged experience with farm life, and the task of teaching me was assigned to Cousin Hiram's son, known as Young Hiram.

"I followed Young Hiram around as he did his chores and tried to work with him. Up at dawn: feed the chickens, slop the hogs, feed the horses, put the cows out to pasture, all before breakfast. Then we were ready for the meal: hot cereal, ham, bacon, eggs, fruit and milk or coffee. In the center of the table, there was a mound of hot biscuits to be eaten with fresh churned butter and homemade preserves or apple butter.

"After breakfast everyone went into the front parlor where Cousin Hiram read from the Bible. His wife, Cousin Virginia, stood beside her husband and their daughter, Young Virginia, played hymns on the organ.

"Then it was back to the fields, plowing furrows: one row this way, one row back. Guiding the plow was hard work. And there was the hay. There were wagons piled high with freshly mown hay followed by the ride to the barn where it was tossed, forkful by forkful, into the hayloft.

"Most fascinating of all was the cider mill. Old Daisy walked the treadmill, pressing layers of sweet apples by turning wheels that propelled the machine. Watching pure apple juice pour down from the presses, I could seldom resist the urge to break off a piece of straw and whet my thirst.

"In those days, when people liked to make their own cider and wine, not everyone was fortunate enough to own a cider mill. But Cousin Hiram's father had one built when he bought his farm after the Civil War.

"He used to make champagne cider that was sold all over the world. Each bottle was carefully wired to restrain the effervescence of fermented juice. If you didn't open it properly, the cork would pop out, spraying everything within range.

"In later years, when the cider mill was no longer in operation, Young Virginia had it converted to a home for herself and her husband. Naturally, it was called Cider Mill House, and you could find it just off Cider Mill Lane, in Lloyd Harbor, New York."

Sara Hewitt Riola
Lakewood, New Jersey

I Always Became Hungry at Grandma's House

When I was a little girl, I loved to go to my Grandma and Grandpa Hill's. They lived on a farm and we lived close to them.

Grandma always had biscuits and molasses and I became very hungry when I went there.

They didn't have a lot of money, but they always had company who enjoyed eating with them. Grandma always set a good table. No matter how many came, there was plenty for all.

Grandpa drove a team of horses and they went to town in a hack, which was kind of like a buggy with no top. I went with them many times.

Before they started out for the long trip, Grandma would run out and grab three or four old fat hens and tie their feet and put them in a sack. Along with her bucket of cream, she took them to the produce store and sold them for coffee, sugar and whatever else she needed.

They kept their milk, butter and cream in a spring near the house. The water kept it all nice and cool. They also had a big garden.

The kinfolk from Kansas City used to come when they got their vacations, and whole families stayed at Grandma's. They had a small log house, but somehow she managed. I don't know where they all slept, but everybody was happy and loved one another. I will always remember going to their house.

Sophie Wood
Eldon, Missouri

Good Times at Our Aunt and Uncle's Farm

Although my sister and I were "town girls," we got to visit our aunt and uncle on their farm for a week or two in the summertime. While there, we were allowed to play in the barn with new kittens or puppies and to gather eggs from the henhouse and barn.

There was a little creek in which to wade, so on a bright sunny day, we might take a picnic lunch, load up the old truck, and my sister and I would enjoy the cool water while our aunt and uncle fixed fences.

We girls had never tasted watercress, but one day we four gathered some near the edge of the creek. I didn't care for the taste of it, but the cool water felt good to my feet as I was picking it. We took the watercress back to the house for salads.

We were warned about the possibility of leeches, ugly little creatures that would suck our blood, so I was continually looking down in the clear water to see if I could see one before it latched onto me. I never saw one, though, for which I was very thankful.

On Saturday morning, we four would go into town to get groceries. One store sold bologna by the stick, so we would get a stick and then we'd have sandwiches when we got home. That night we would go to a movie in town. It cost only a dime for each person, whether they were a child or an adult. Before the main movie was shown, there was a serial, which ended in an exciting way to make a person want to return the following Saturday night and see more.

By the side of their garden, my aunt and uncle had black raspberries, and we enjoyed them as we picked them. Blackberries grew in the fields, which we also enjoyed. We thought there was nothing finer than berries heaped with sugar and lots of thick, creamy milk. We would watch as their many cows were moved into the barn and milked by hand. The waiting cats would catch a stream of milk, then drink from pans until their fat little tummies were full. We would go into the "separator house" where the milk and cream were separated by a machine. They sold cream in town in large cream cans, as well as eggs by the crates.

A huge rectangular concrete stock tank was used to water the cows. My sister and I enjoyed playing in the cool water. I'm sure we were not always clean, but the cows never complained about the "stirred-up" water.

Both my aunt and uncle are gone now, but my sister and I have many happy memories of fun on the farm.

Colleen Agee
Houston, Missouri

Enjoying the Wide-Open Spaces

My brother and I were both born at home in the mid-1930s. Times were hard in the country, so Dad and Mom decided we should move to town. Dad got a job in town making $15 a week. His dad told him, "Son you are going to get rich." In 1928, after farming for one year, my granddad cleared $5 after making the $14 per year payment on the farm.

Our grandparents raised their own pork and corn. My grandma smoked pork meat in the smokehouse and just smelling it cook would "make your tongue slap your brains out." The corn bread was delicious too. It was cooked in a long metal pan, and when you put that fresh country butter on it, you just didn't know when to quit eating.

My brother and I always enjoyed visiting our grandparents. We liked the country because we could enjoy the wide open spaces. In town, you just didn't have room to move around like kids have to do. My parents didn't own an automobile. In town, you just rode a bus, for which the fare was only one nickel. They would rent a car for the day's visit to the country and my brother and I would stay a week or two whenever we could.

From the beginning, I always called my dad's parents my granddad and my grandmother. My mother's parents were my brother's granddad and grandma. Everyone who knew us got a kick out of hearing me say I was going to my brother's grandparents or hearing him say he was going to mine.

After we were old enough to travel the 30 miles on the bus by ourselves, we would go to visit our grandparents. The bus traveled the main highway, leaving us a mile and a half to travel by foot on the dusty or muddy road. We would get to my brother's grandparents' house first, so I would spend the night with them. The next day, I would make another mile-and-a-half trip to get to my grandparents. Sometimes I made the walk alone and sometimes my brother would go with me. My granddad had a car, so when my brother wanted to go back to his grandparents, my granddad and I would get the old Model A Ford and take him to their house.

My grandpa lived to be 76 years of age; my grandma lived to age 75. My brother's granddad lived to age 75 and his grandma to age 80. The good Lord gave two boys lots of really good times with their grandparents.

Hollis G. Jones
Eclectic, Alabama

Memories Live On

The yearly trek to Missouri from the Colorado dust bowl plains in the late 1920s and early '30s was always something for me to look forward to. It was a straight-line journey through the state of Kansas, where the grasshoppers would land on the car's hood emblem and I would want my dad to go faster and get ahead of them—I can still hear him laugh! There was no air conditioner in the car, but I do remember stopping and getting drinks of water at windmills along the way. We all drank from the long-handled dipper that was attached to the windmill's frame—I don't remember my mother ever worrying about us getting any disease by drinking from the public dipper. There weren't any rest stops or bathrooms either.

Grandpa's barking dog announced our arrival. Grandpa would amble out and ask my dad how much he paid for his new car before we ever got out. I don't remember Grandmother coming out; she was always standing with open arms inside the kitchen.

She was short and fat, always wearing a long dress, her hair pulled up in a knot and standing firm in her lady "somebody" shoes. Her face was creased with wrinkles, her hands worn by many years of hard work, but as she pressed you to her bosom you only felt love and comfort and contentment.

The old black cookstove had the coffeepot on, and the massive buffet held Grandpa's cookies and bread. Daddy used to get Mother to wash the inside of the coffeepot really good as he said the coffee was so strong (they never threw out the grounds—just added more along with some eggshells), and Grandpa would swear up and down that the coffee wasn't fit to drink.

I really don't remember what we had to eat while we were there. I do remember when Grandpa would lather the old white oleo (before it had the yellow capsule you mixed in) on a piece of bread about an inch thick—it made me think of someone plastering a house. The spoon holder with the grape design that sat on the table graces my table now.

West of the farm a tiny little brook ran through a grove of persimmon trees. We played in the grass and the little pebbles in the brook while the many birds serenaded my brother and me. We built boats out of leaves and scraps of tree bark and played many make-believe games. What a contrast that little grove of trees, the singing brook and the grass were to where we lived in Colorado. Sixty years later I went looking for that oasis. It was no longer there—and neither were my grandparents.

Sometimes we were there when they were cutting feed, and I remember the oat bugs being terrible one time. As you perspired—there were no air conditioners or fans then—those tiny bugs attached themselves to you; they got in your ears, eyes and nose and made you miserable. I can still see Grandmother taking two of the dining chairs, spreading them about six feet apart with backs toward each other and tying a sheet across, making me a "house where the bugs won't find you." What a great Grandmother she was to a tiny girl.

I used to love to gather the eggs, much to the consternation of my grandfather. Whenever I would bring in a soft-shelled egg he would go into a complete tizzy. He was so positive that I was "scaring the eggs out of the hens and not letting them take their time in laying them," never realizing that he wasn't feeding them a balanced diet!

Probably at about the age of 6 I decided that I wanted to ride bareback on a young colt Grandpa had. I had no fear of anything at that age—still don't—and I took off down the lane at a leisurely pace. What I didn't know was that when I turned that colt around that it was going to go home like a speeding bullet! I hung on for dear life and the colt was running so close to a barbed wire fence that I thought for sure my leg was going to be gone. My dad was watching my "trip" and immediately closed the barn door so the colt wouldn't knock me off when it went in. I was "saved by the bell." That little trip earned me the nickname of "Stormy," as the colt had been born on a stormy night and that was its name.

Sixty-seven years of marriage were celebrated in that house before Grandfather died and Grandmother went to live in town. The grove of trees and my brook are gone but the memories are not. Now when I go to Missouri, I go to the cemetery, clean their stones, leave flowers and silently thank them for what I have. I still see Grandmother in the kitchen, tears running down her cheeks and her ample bosom, shaking from laughter because I had latched the screen door and Grandpa couldn't get in—he could sure holler loud!

Jean L. Robinson
Mesa, Arizona

———■———

INDEX